*Dear —
I hope you enjoy* Love —
as much as I enjoyed Catherine M. Troost
together.

CATSKILL MOUNTAIN
MEMORIES

Catherine M. Troost

xulon
PRESS

PREFACE

L et me start first with a story of our move to the
country through the eyes, and from the thoughts
of a five and a half year old girl (with the mind of a
ten year old).

NANCY MOVES TO THE MOUNTAINS

As Nancy was hugging her little friend, Linda,
while saying good-bye, she was excited, but yet, not
sure of her emotional feelings. After all, the two five-
year-old girls grew up together in the same neighborhood, but here she was, leaving her friend for good.
Nancy's family had decided to pull out of the north-
central community of Carteret, New Jersey, and
move up to the Catskill Mountains in upstate New
York, outside of the village of East Meredith. But,
at almost six years old, Nancy thought of it as just
another vacation for a week or two. She and Linda
were already making plans for when they would be
together again.

"Mom said you can visit me up in the mountains soon, Linda," said Nancy. "Maybe you can come sometime in the summer."

As Linda was thinking that over, she realized then what that meant. "Aren't you going to come back for school?" she asked.

Nancy's Mom explained that Nancy will be going to a new school. "We'll send you and your Mom a letter or two and keep in touch about our farm, and make plans for you to visit, O.K.?"

Linda gave Nancy a little hug and then watched as her friend climbed into the back of the green station-wagon. Nancy's little two-year old brother, Tom, and baby sister, Cathy, were already in with her Aunt Nancy and cousin, Sharon.

Nancy's Dad had left earlier in their other car with her older brothers, Billy and Eddie. Following them were Uncle Marty and Uncle Richie with the big truck that was rented for the weekend, loaded with furniture and all of their belongings.

As her Mom got into the driver's seat, she said, "Children, you know this trip will take at least five or six hours, so I'd like you to settle down with your books and crayons and games. It will make the driving much easier for me."

Brother Tommy excitedly chattered about the cows he remembered seeing in the mountains when the family visited the place they were moving to. Little Cathy was content in the car-bed with her bottle of milk. Finally, Tommy started to scribble in his coloring book after Mom had been driving a while. Nancy watched out the window as they headed for the highway, passing by the familiar houses and stores that she saw when riding the school-bus. Turning onto the highway, Nancy became a bit anxious as they left their town, finally realizing that she wouldn't be seeing these sights again for a long time. Tears started to well up in her big, blue eyes. The past few weeks had been so exciting, thinking of the big move to the mountains, but now....

"Hey diddle, diddle, the cat and the fiddle," sang Aunt Nancy. "The cow jumped over the moon!"

Three-year-old Sharon, and Tommy joined in, "the little dog laughed to see such sport...."

"And the dish ran away with the spoon!" chimed in Nancy and Mom.

"Let's sing some more, Aunt Nancy!" said Tommy. "Baa, baa, black sheep, have you any wool?"

Nancy relaxed as they sang. Even Mom's driving was more relaxed. After several songs, Aunt Nancy started a game. "Let's all choose a color," she said, "and see who can count the most cars in an hour."

Mom helped Tommy with his color - red. They counted up to twenty-two red cars. Of course, Tommy became all mixed up with his numbers after five, so was happy he had Mom to help. Aunt Nancy and Sharon counted fifteen green cars, including the station-wagon. But, with Mom's help, Nancy counted twenty-eight blue cars. She knew she would win! Blue was her favorite color.

Two hours had already passed by, and Cathy had awakened and was getting fussy. Mom came to a rest area along the highway and parked near a picnic table. There was a large shaded spot near-by with swings and a sliding board. Nancy raced to the sliding board with Tommy and Sharon right behind her. Two blond braids were bouncing as she climbed the ladder to the top. It felt so good to get out of that car!! Mom changed Cathy's diaper as Aunt Nancy spread a cloth on the table and unpacked the picnic basket. Over a half hour passed by as they played and ate the lunch Mom had made for the long trip.

"You have ten minutes to finish playing, kids, then we have to get going again!" Mom called.

Back in the car, Nancy thought, "Oh, I'm going to get so bored counting cars again with Aunt Nancy! Only she'll probably have us count cows or horses this time."

It was a good thing Mom let her bring her favorite pillow because within ten minutes Nancy had fallen asleep. When she awoke, her eyes opened wide! Up ahead and passing on either side of the road they were on, were huge mountains. Nancy still couldn't believe that she was going to live in the middle of mountains and farms. As she looked at the others, Tommy and Cathy were sleeping. Aunt Nancy's head was bobbing, as was her cousin, Sharon's, head, which was sleeping on her Mom's lap.

"Mom," Nancy whispered, will it be much longer?"

"We're almost there, dear. Don't be too impatient. I know it's been a long day for you - for all of us," Mom said, as she turned off the highway.

"Oh, no, Mom, I'm not really impatient. I just want to see the place before it gets dark."

"It won't be dark for quite awhile, Nancy. We've only a few more miles to go."

Nancy tried to read the book she brought along. The book Linda gave her as a 'going - away' present. She thought about the party Linda's Mom had for the family. The whole neighborhood was there to wish them well with their move. Nancy thought of Barbie and Carol who were almost as close to her as Linda. She remembered the men shaking hands with her Dad and brothers, and the women kissing the whole family.

She remembered, too, how Mom and Dad talked to her and her older brothers one night of their decision to move to the mountains. They thought it would be best in the country, away from the bustling, growing city life that seemed to be getting too 'tight' for them to live in. Nancy wasn't sure of what that meant. Everyone seemed to like the whole idea though. Nancy's daydreaming stopped when Tommy and Cathy woke up.

"We're almost there, Tommy!" she exclaimed.

Just then, Mom turned the station-wagon into the long driveway.

"Is this it!" asked Aunt Nancy. "It's just beautiful!! And look! Snow flakes are starting to fall!"

The big white farmhouse was beyond a small pond on one side of the driveway. An apple orchard was on the other side. Nancy's Dad, Uncle Richie, and Uncle Marty had already arrived and were unloading the truck. Billy and Eddie were anxious to go exploring, but were dutifully helping with the boxes and smaller pieces of furniture. As Mom turned off the car, everyone seemed to jump out at once, (except Cathy).

"What big trees! And the house is so big! Do you think we could all have our own bedrooms, Mom?"

"Nancy, we'll just have to wait and see."

Nancy and her mother walked into the kitchen and were surprised to see a gallon of milk on the counter. Along with it was a package of ground meat, a large bowl of frozen peas, and two jars of home-made applesauce. Next to all of that was a big choco-late cake!

"The only people who could have left such food as this are the ones who were taking care of the place for us from the farm down the road. And here's a note saying 'welcome home, enjoy!' What wonderful neighbors!" Mom declared. "This will taste so much better than the sandwiches and canned soup I was planning on. Nancy, help your Aunt to find the box of pots and pans; we'll have a real supper! I haven't had homemade applesauce in a long, long time. This is such a wonderful treat and surprise!"

Nancy couldn't believe that people who hardly knew her family could be so kind and thoughtful. She wondered if they had any children around her age.

It was well into the evening and everyone was truly tired. The hot supper Mom had made satisfied everyone. Most of the furniture was in place, and there were extra mattresses on the large living room floor where Nancy's two uncles would sleep. Aunt Nancy and Sharon had a room upstairs where they would be staying for several weeks to help Mom get adjusted, and keep her company since Nancy's Dad had to leave in a week to go back to his job in New Jersey till he found one here in the mountains. Her two uncles would stay another day, but then had to get the truck back the day after.

The older boys and Nancy had explored most of the farm before supper, and had even run over to the big pond across the road. Billy and Eddie were excited about the fish they had seen jumping, but Dad had said tomorrow would be soon enough to unpack the fishing gear.

Mr. And Mrs. Meyers, the neighbor farmers, had come after their milking chores were done. Mom and Dad could hardly thank them enough for all they had done; especially for building the fire in the huge furnace in the cellar and warming up the house.... and cleaning and dusting it. And the food was a wonderful plus!!

Nancy and her brothers went to bed after the Meyers went home. Cathy was asleep in her crib, sharing the same room with Nancy - but she didn't mind. It was different having an upstairs bedroom. The house they left that morning had all the rooms on one floor.

Before falling off to sleep, Nancy thought of all that had happened. Leaving a busy city, leaving all her friends.... She wondered about new friends, a new teacher, a new school. How different it will be without sidewalks and traffic lights. There didn't seem to be any cars out on the road in front of their farmhouse. She thought of the fish in the pond, wading in the stream, running through the fields. She thought of the animals Dad and Mom planned on....

chickens, ducks, pigs, calves....maybe a cute pony. At least a puppy!

"Goodness," Nancy thought. "I better get some sleep! What was it Mrs. Meyers told me? They have three boys and two girls, too, just like our family. The girls are older, but she will ask them to show me around their farm. And how to milk cows. Oh! And they have a mama pig with six babies! And two horses! We'll ride on the hay wagon, too. In the spring we can pick wild strawberries. And there are many blueberry bushes in the fields. I've only ever helped Mom pick out a nice basket of strawberries at the store. When Linda comes for her vacation I'll have so much to show her, I won't know where to begin!"

Nancy finally drifted off to sleep to awaken to a bright new day.

Chapter 1

CATSKILL MOUNTAIN MEMORIES

Learning to live in the country… outdoors, and in!!

Memories of the Catskill Mountains keep flooding my mind. When my husband, Bill, and I first pulled away from our very busy suburban life in north central New Jersey, back in the 1960's, my father-in-law asked if we knew we were moving back fifty years in "progress". We knew. We uprooted our five young children, three boys, aged 12, 10, and 1 and ½, and two girls, one aged 5 years and the other, 6 months. In the middle of 'no-where', we planted new roots up in the Catskill Mountains of New York State, a virtual paradise for raising children.

Settling into a large abandoned farmhouse that we bought, we became used to Winter quickly since we moved in the middle of January! Being pampered by piped-in city gas that supplied our radiant heat through the floors of our home in New Jersey, it took a while to learn to keep our slippers or shoes on in the old house that just had a huge coal furnace in the cellar which sent the heat up into the only floor register in the middle of the main hall that connected all the downstairs rooms. At the far end of the long living room there was a wood-burning stove. For some reason, I called it George because its handle looked like a big cigar. There was a smaller wood stove in the upstairs hallway that was supposed to warm the five bedrooms.

That first winter there was a day when we all went to the town of Oneonta (which was fifteen miles away), to do some shopping. We forgot to stoke the furnace! We came home to find a frozen water pipe had burst and water was running across the kitchen floor. The furnace fire had gone out!! Bill had to quickly find wood and logs to start the initial fire before he could shovel coal onto it. We surely learned a lesson that day!

Needing to keep a tight budget, we had only allotted so much money for the coal supply, never realizing that first Winter season just how much coal we would be using! We didn't realize how long the winters would be either. With the coal running out before hand, we had to go into our nearby woods to look for downed, dried trees to saw and chop, and bring back to the house, usually on sleds or tobog- gans through drifted snow. Oh, my, did our older boys dislike that job. The only time they didn't mind going out for wood was in early spring when we collected sap and boiled it down for maple syrup so they could sell it to earn money.

Thinking now of a few years later, I chuckle at the time when one of the boys decided to raise three little pigs to earn money. They became his pets. They'd come to him when he gave a special whistle. They also knew the squeaking sound of the feed pail handle when he'd feed them. One morning while he was in school, the pigs broke out of their pen. I saw the three of them scurrying up the tractor path and on into the meadow. I whistled for them. I made the squeaky noise with the feed pail, trying to get them to turn around and follow me. They ran the other way, and it seemed as if they were laughing at me! There was no one else at home. The kids were at school, my husband was at work. What else could I do but go to the school and embarrass my son by asking his teacher to excuse him to help me round up his pigs. "To do what???" she asked. Being in farm country, she understood. All he had to do was give his knowing whistle, call their names, jiggle the pail, and the three little pigs came running right out of the fields toward him and into the barn! I did have my son back to school by lunchtime. Although he didn't want to go back with his face so red from embarrassment!

Another memory was of going out into the woods for a Christmas tree. The biggest and prettiest was always the one furthest away. Our neighbor farmer helped drag our first tree out with his tractor. It was so huge! He just laughed at us, knowing the tree was too big to get into the house. We had to take several feet off the trunk and two more off the top! But we all thought it was the most beautiful tree worthy of Jesus' birthday.

During the summer the children would get a little bored with each other (as many children do). They had animals to take care of, gardens to weed, a stream to explore, a pond to fish and swim in, but they still needed something more. There was an organization in New York City called the Fresh Air Fund. It was for under-privileged kids to give them a week or two to vacation in the mountains. I applied for a boy and a girl each year. This would keep our kids busy for a couple weeks. We also had a young niece from New Jersey that would spend the summer with us. Very often other relatives and friends would come for a week or so to vacation in the beautiful mountains. We had quite a bit of acreage for them to all run around in and enjoy themselves. But I especially remember the Fresh Air city kids. Their eyes would open wide when they first saw the fields and dirt roads and paths without fear of any street traffic. They would get a little nervous when camping outside, being so dark with only a security light shining. Of course, porch lights were left on and some lights inside the house. The idea that toys, bicycles, or garden tools could be left outside overwhelmed them. Wouldn't someone come and steal them? One summer a young nephew was visiting from New Jersey. There was a day when he helped me collect eggs from the chicken coop. After that, when he wouldn't eat eggs any more, I asked him why not? His reply? "Because they came from the dirty nests and floor of the coop!! My Mom buys clean eggs from the grocery store!"

The memories are many of the Catskills. Ice-skating on the pond, tobogganing down the snowy slopes of the fields, climbing our own apple trees to harvest the beautiful red fruit, going out in the fields and woodland edges to pick gallons of wild blueberries, and then stuffing ourselves, and visitors, with blueberry muffins and pies. As afternoon showers came over the mountains and passed by, there would usually be a wonderful rainbow, and we'd wonder which end to follow to find that fabled pot of gold.

Then there were the birds. In the wintertime keeping the chickadees, nuthatches, and blue jays fed was a delightful chore. But in March, when I would hear the first red-winged blackbird out in the meadow, I knew that long-awaited springtime was on the way. Shortly after that would come a bold robin or two. They would huddle under the pines during the snow showers. Then flocks of redwings would drift in with grackles and brown-headed cowbirds. Once in awhile a flash of blue would signal in the bluebirds. Tree swallows, barn swallows, evening grosbeaks, cedar waxwings - I couldn't keep up with all the bird watching I wanted to do! Catching a glimpse of a deer with her new fawn trotting after her was also a sight to see in the Spring.

During the years that followed, changes were taking place. Farmlands became vacant. People from the 'city' came and started to build their vacation homes. Department and large grocery stores were beating out the small main street country stores. Perhaps we did go back about fifty years in progress, as my father-in-law had said, when we moved to the

Catskills back in the 60's, but we enjoyed those many years when we stepped back in time. Eventually progress caught up with us, or was it that we caught up with progress? Our children still reminisce of growing up in the country, and my husband and I never regretted our move to the Catskill Mountains. Those memories will be with us wherever we go!

One thing our children didn't know until years later was how 'strapped' we were in the financial department. Living in one of the more destitute counties of New York State (Delaware County) at that time, our kids' friends, who came from farming families, probably didn't realize either. Most of the children knew that after school there were chores to do, and homework, and then time to go out and enjoy the countryside. In high school most took up sports to release their high energy. For Bill and I, it was one of the hardest things to stretch the pay-check - especially when it was not as much as the one earned in New Jersey, and the mortgage was more than we were paying back in New Jersey....and raising five kids took the cake! And the icing! And the iced cream!!! But, looking back at the struggles and hardships, the good times out-weighed it all!

Needless to say, as the children grew old enough, my husband and I taught them all that was needed to know about hunting and fishing. We learned how to raise our own beef, pork, and chicken; so we knew how to clean and butcher. Through the years, as the children emptied the proverbial nest, they have drifted to other states. Only the oldest son still lives in the Catskills with his wife and family. He is still enjoying the mountains, the four seasons, and the hunting and fishing. As for myself, I am now a retired widow, enjoying the warm, suburban life in Florida.

We did have many ups and downs, but those stories are for another time to write. Let me reminisce and record some stories that I'm sure young and old would appreciate. One of my favorite memories of the Catskills is about shooting country wildlife.

Chapter 2.

SHOOTING COUNTRY WILDLIFE

I f you think this is about hunting and using a gun, relax, it isn't. As I became older, I lost interest in that type of hunting. One beautiful spring day, late in the afternoon, I was walking the fields with our family dog, part collie, called Mr. Love, (of all names). My new camera that Bill gave me as a Christmas present was slung over my shoulder. The dog and I went through an opening in a stone wall, which the Catskills are famous for, and sat on a knoll in the field beyond.

All of a sudden, there was Katt! My white cat with black spots was walking along the top of the stone wall. I hadn't realized he had followed us. Then, there was a flash of something brown below the knoll coming from an old apple orchard. I made the collie lie down. He obeyed, nervously. We watched in silence as a young deer, its faded spots barely visible, pranced out into the open field, curiously eyeing Katt. As Katt was softly padding along the wall in my direction, the deer seemed to tiptoe toward him, as if it had never seen a cat before (but then, perhaps it never had!). With the deer's eyes riveted on Katt, I was able to slowly reach for the camera and get the deer and the cat into focus. By then the sun was setting and trees shaded everything. The deer's keen ears picked up the click of the camera. When it looked in my direction it heeled and bounded back to the orchard with startled determination. It was all I could do to hold onto Mr. Love's collar, who, by then, was so excited that he wanted to race after the young animal.

The developed picture was as I had expected, mostly dark shadows. The white blob of Katt was there, but the deer was just a brown blur. With that exciting moment I was hooked. I became an amateur shooter of wildlife....with a camera. Living in a secluded area with fields and woods and nearby streams I saw many species of wildlife. Every once in a while a doe would come into view, usually with a set of young, spotted twin fawns. The young ones, filled with curiosity, would prance over to the bird feeders hung in the trees out on the lawn, and they would look in amazement as the birds took their fill of seeds.

Then, at other times, the red or gray squirrels would come up on the deck to check out the grill to see and smell what we may have had for dinner the night before. I was able to get a few shots of them with their nose going into the holes near the handles.

Sometimes they were able to reach the bird feeders and knock them so the seeds would fall to the ground. Then it was a race to see who got to the fallen seeds, since the chipmunks hid under the deck just waiting for handouts. I have used many rolls of film trying to get the right angle at the right moment....but with very little luck. I did get a shot of a gray squirrel that was able to tightrope walk to a bird feeder that was tied to a clothesline. It tried to chew off the hook so it would drop to the ground, but that didn't work. The squirrel then hung upside down to get at the seeds.

Have you ever seen or heard hummingbirds as they fight and chase each other from their feeders? What a riot!! A dominant male usually sits on the clothesline that the feeder with its nectar is tied to, making sure that no other hummer comes for a drink. When he goes off looking for gnats, a brave young male will sneak in for a sip. Zoom! The older male comes back and dive-bombs the intruder. He dives at most of the other hummers that try to drink, except for an occasional female.

There are times when I wish I had infrared flashes. I have seen raccoons come up on the lawn during the evening. These little masked creatures are cutely curious as they hop on the deck and then go to the feeders. They pick up anything they can get their hands - I mean paws - on. They check under the picnic table and benches for any morsel available. They scavenge under the apple trees for fallen fruit. But their biggest puzzle is how to get to those feeders on the clothesline.

While going for a walk one day after a snowfall, I saw a ball of fur nesting in the bare branches of a small tree. As I walked closer to the tree the fur ball seemed to expand. Then I got yet a little closer, and, whoa!! I really wanted to run!! It was a porcupine! Was it chewing the tree bark or was it just enjoying the warm sun? Collecting my wits and my nerve, I got as close as I wanted, and, believe it or not, it was very accommodating, and let me shoot with my camera. It seemed rather pleased that I didn't bother him any more than I did, and it decided to curl up again and finish its nap. To me, they were some exciting moments!

Shooting in the Catskills with my camera became much more adventuresome and rewarding. I've taken pictures of wild turkeys, deer, hawks, all from my front door or open window, but most were not very clear. A shot that I would have been ecstatic to get is of the bobcat that hung around the mountain. I had only seen it twice, and it was quite large, healthy, and beautiful. I think it would have been a better idea for the hunters to go out in the woods and fields each season of the year with a camera to shoot wildlife. What nicer pictures to have than that of the ten-point buck, or the black bear. And then there was the elusive pileated woodpecker. Also, trying to bring in that V-formation of Canada geese with a zoom lens was a job. I never became a professional photographer, but it was a bunch of fun trying to shoot Catskill Mountain wildlife.

Chapter 3

BUT DEER DON'T EAT GREEN TOMATOES!

Before moving to the Catskills my husband would go deer hunting in northern New Jersey. We lived in north central New Jersey in a very crowded suburban town. Usually, the night before he'd go hunting I would find myself sewing big bright red patches on his old winter jacket. He never wanted to have me buy him a new hunting jacket or hat or boots since that would peg him as one of those "city" hunters. Off he would go 50 or 60 miles to a friend's farm where he would look like his friend does, living in the back woods. If the deer were not on the friend's farm it was easy for them to get permission to do their trespassing on other farmland by the way they looked. They were never turned away.

If I remember correctly, he only bagged two deer during the ten years of hunting in the north Jersey woodlands.

When our town was really bursting at the seams, and our little plot of ground with our small ranch home became the neighborhood playground, I wasn't about to become the convenient, gratuitous, neighborhood baby sitter. I loved my neighbors, but sitting my own five children was just about enough! Besides, I was brought up on a New Jersey farm and I longed once again for the wide-open spaces. After all my whimpering, and complaining, and threatening, my poor husband gave up his secure job as a policeman and let me have my way. (How many husbands would give in like that??)

We dug up our roots, as mentioned before, and planted them in 500 acres of abandoned farmland which included an old farmhouse, a large barn, and several run down barns, on the western slopes of the Catskills in New York State. Now this was back when an acre of land was only ten or twenty bucks - dollars, that is. As for real bucks, it wasn't unusual to see three or four each night under the apple trees in front of the house. They would be accompanied by their families of several does and little fawns. A beautiful sight! We moved up in January and it was quite hard to wait for the big game season that first year - but, wait we did. Our 'city' friends thought us foolish. Who'd see us smack in the middle of 500 acres? The only traffic we ever saw was the school bus, a snowplow, and the mailman's jeep. It sure was tempting! But, come November that first year, there I was, sewing those red patches back on the winter jacket once again. This time we really couldn't afford new hunting outfits!!

The large sprawling farmhouse was turned into a hunting lodge each year during the big game season. We would have between twelve and sixteen hunters each day for two weeks. It took a lot of ham and eggs and toast and coffee to get a bunch like that ready to go into the fields and woods for the day. Only they didn't stay out for the day. By the time the breakfast dishes were done (we had no dish washer back then), and the beds made, they'd be back for mid-morning coffee break. Even though I had packed lunches for them to eat in the field, they would all be back by noon to have hot coffee and/or soup, to warm up, and then sit around the big old oval oak table and talk and boast about the one that got away, or that they almost got. Then they would plan their strategies for the afternoon, like a big drive through the swamp or up over the mountain. Some of the guys would just decide to take a nap since that's what they thought the deer would be doing in the afternoon anyway. They would then go out just before sundown.

In the evening, over a twenty-pound roast turkey or ham, or both, heaps of mashed potatoes, and the rest of the trimmings, chocolate cakes, apple pies; they would once again talk of the one that got away (with a rack that was twice as big as the one of the morning). I considered it all fun as long as it was only for two weeks. The money was good, and the kids received nice tips for taking the luggage up and down the stairs. The luggage consisted of bright red hunting outfits, usually brand new, two or three pairs of hunting boots for each hunter, and at least two or three rifles each. This never seemed to bother my friend, husband, who kept wearing an old jacket with new bright red patches sewed onto it. The hunters were rather fortunate going home with their game tied to their vehicles. They seemed to like the place since they kept coming back each year. They also liked it since they knew they'd be paying double at other hunting lodges.

If I remember correctly, my husband only bagged two deer during his ten years of hunting at this farmstead.

Eventually, we realized we couldn't hold on to the farm. The kids were getting older, the needs to raise them became more demanding, college was playing in their minds, so we either had to sell out or go bankrupt. We found a nice little farmette with fifteen acres in the same county about twenty-five miles away. It was much closer to where my husband worked, making it more convenient for him to travel over the mountains. He had been very fortunate in finding a job as soon as we had moved up to the big farm. He had always warned me that he was not a farmer, so we had used the place for our own enjoyment, raising animals and gardens only for our own consumption. His job was being a supervisor at a state school for teenage delinquent boys. This job was more rewarding to him than being a policeman. The new farm (new to us) had a lovely home, but only big enough for our own family. This meant no extra hunters. Our three boys made up for them. As they became of age, they each received their hunting license. When our youngest son took his hunting test,

I decided it was time for me to take one. I passed! Our two girls eventually became licensed, also.

On our little farm we raised some beef cows, a couple of pigs and a few chickens each year. But, my enjoyment was gardening. The digging, the planting, even the weeding was fun for me, and certainly, the harvesting. Our freezers were always full of meat and veggies. Toward the end of each summer there were a lot of green tomatoes left. We would get our fill of red ripe tomatoes in salads, in stews, in soups, in sauces, in canning jars, in the freezer! Then there would be fried green tomatoes, green tomato pickles, green tomato relish, green tomato jams, and still green tomatoes left in the garden. Each fall I would notice that some green tomatoes would be half eaten in the garden. Not that I cared, I was just curious about it.

My husband would say, "The woodchucks are filling up for their winter hibernation."

I would say, "The bites are too big for wood-chucks, it has to be the deer."

He would say, "Oh, no, deer don't eat green tomatoes!"

"They must!" I'd say.

"But they don't!" he'd say.

Another year on this farm as I was again harvesting vegetables, I noticed the deer hoof prints going down some of the rows. I wonder if they were surprised when they bit into one particular squash and it came out like strings of spaghetti. Actually, the spaghetti squash is very tasty with the sauce I made from the tomatoes. I also found several sizes of the two-pointed hoof prints, indicative of deer, around the green tomatoes that were bitten into.

Again he said, "But deer don't eat green tomatoes!"

One year I had the privilege of receiving a doe permit. Everyone does not get these permits. You have to apply for them, and then just a few are chosen. It was a perfect morning when I went out to fill my permit. The ground had a light snow covering. I went out behind the barn, and there it was, just waiting for me. After my husband helped me with field dressing the animal (he's good that way), we dragged it back to the house. As we did, we followed the tracks it had made in the snow, noticing that they came from the garden. It had been pawing in the snow around the old tomato plants that never got tilled into the ground.

I just had to make one last remark. "Dear, you know as well as I do that this deer was looking for one last green tomato before it met its end!!"

If I remember correctly, my husband only bagged two deer during the ten years we lived at this home!!!

Chapter 4

WATCHING FOR BIRDS

An engrossing pastime for me was when I became enamored with bird watching. I would sit at the picnic table and look out over the field beyond the dirt road going past our place. A near-by farmer always kept the field mowed and used the hay for his heifers on his farm about two miles away. The red-winged blackbirds seemed to always have a few scouts flying above, because as soon as the last bale of hay was taken away on the hay wagon, a flock would come in and start scavenging the field for the seeds left behind. They would stay in the field to eat, and then practice flight maneuvers. It was time for flocking up and get ready for their long flight south. There would be approximately fifty in the flock, but then each day ten or more would join up. Soon, after a few days, there seemed to be more than a hundred. It was amazing to see how they could play follow the leader. In flight the redwings would bank to the left, then to the right, over the electric high wires. One or two more semi-loops up toward the mountain, and back they came to land in the field.

Each day as I would sit outside and watch them, the flock seemed to grow. Once in a while I could get my husband and other family members to watch their amazing flight patterns, but football season was starting and most of the time I'd be sitting by myself enjoying this truly wondrous gift of God, of birds in flight. The redwings would practice for almost a month, as their flock would continue to build up. The maneuvers were astounding, especially as they seemed to know how to bank, swirl, climb, and dive, all at one time, together. They would land and feed on the weed seeds, and rest, and take off again. One day I would go out to the picnic table and not hear a thing, nor see a redwing, and then I knew. They were gone till the next year.

Another time I walked behind our old barn to the stone wall and tree line that divided the fields in back of our farm. I heard a not too familiar twitter. What was it? Finally, in a choke-cherry tree I saw Carolina chickadees....smaller than our usual black capped chickadees. They didn't spot me as they kept flitting around the leaves, having tasty snacks of tiny insects imbedded on the undersides of the leaves. Then I saw the inconspicuous rose-breasted grosbeak scratching up the leaves on the ground. He didn't think I saw him, but the rosy hue on his breast gave him away. He was too busy looking for grubs, which he finally found, for his two young ones perched up on the beech tree. The young have a soft, almost eerie, monotone call as they wait for the mushy morsels from their parent. The female must have been elsewhere looking for more tidbits to bring them.

As I would sit on the stone wall I reveled in all that God was presenting for me to take in. I could hear the robins, bobolinks, mourning doves, and goldfinches in the near distance about me. Many years before I only knew the most common birds; robins, blue jays, crows, sparrows. Now, if I hadn't seen at least nine different sparrows each year, I would have been disappointed! Years before, if I had a few crusts left from an old loaf of bread, the birds were lucky to get them. Now, I was buying pounds and pounds of seeds to put in feeders, and during the winters I was putting out suet here and there. I'd grow rows of sunflowers so the birds could have an early winter treat, especially the blue jays. The hummingbird feeders were replenished every week with their sugar water. The hummers were always fun to watch.

Years before I never thought of birdhouses. The birds were capable in building their own nests in the trees and in the barns, so I thought. Eventually, I had a small house hanging in the apple tree that a family of wrens took over right away. The house hanging in the pine tree was always fought over by tree swallows. A birdhouse was nailed onto the tree in the front yard, and a family of tree swallows swooped in to take claim of it. A pair of my favorite birds, bluebirds, had nested in the new house that was tacked on to the young maple tree. Bluebirds are quiet and unobtrusive, but there are times that they get what they want. This particular pair wanted that new house on that maple tree! They withstood the demanding tree swallows. They let it be known to the pesky starlings that they weren't moving. The arrogant catbird fought with them because he didn't want them living so close to the bush where he and his mate were nesting. The bluebirds stood their ground. I promised them to put up more new houses like that one the following year for when they brought back their young family. Eventually, there were four houses around the lawn and gardens that the bluebirds enjoyed.

Perhaps you might think bird watching is 'for the birds'. Perhaps it is. But it is such a relaxing pastime. As I watched them, gone were the cares of the day - of the world. I didn't think of household chores, gardening, writing, the mundane things that had to be done. An amateur bird-watcher, such as I was, just needs a good bird book, binoculars, notebook, and a pencil. It's fun just to jot down what birds you notice and the time of year. I used to average fifty different birds on my property alone. I did spy other birds in other areas and would also note them on a separate page of the notebook, such as the great blue heron, the pileated woodpecker, the bald eagle, wood thrush, vireo, indigo bunting, and a few others that I saw within a five mile radius of my home.

Even though I am not in the Catskills any more, I still do a good amount of bird watching. And you can, also, no matter where you are. As the sun comes up, the birds become very melodic before they start their busy-ness of the day. Sit out on your back lawn or where ever you have a bit of space. Listen to the different notes of the wrens, the purple finch, the house finch, the song sparrows, and robins. What a musical treat. The barn swallows sit on the wires and chatter away. The grackle gives off a guttural, throaty sound to its young as it takes off to find some breakfast. A downy woodpecker is pecking and looking for its morning meal. Then, in the evening, the sounds are quite different. The birds give forth with softer notes, as if singing lullabies to each other. Of course, you have to listen carefully, because it could all be interrupted with an occasional vehicle going along on the road, or some animal trotting down the lane. The thing that used to interrupt my evening reverie of bird-song was my white cat named Katt. He would come home in the early evening from his hunts in the fields and the frenzy would begin. The wary notes of the parent birds to their young could be heard. Katt was immune to the noise and dive-bombing of the swallows. He was interested in his hunt for snakes, mice, and moles, but, more important, was his coming home and being fed, like a king, in the kitchen with his daily 'meow' mix and bowl of milk.

Birding is a constant source of relaxation and wonderment. It's nice to start the day with their music on your mind, and to share the evening with their notes of solitude. Go to a quiet place. Soon your eyes and ears will be filled in amazement.

Chapter 5

THE TREES OF THE FIELD CLAP THEIR HANDS.

My life became quite busy after moving up into the Catskill Mountains. There was much work mixed in with what we thought was an ideal vacationland. Sure, there was hiking, swimming, ball playing, or tobogganing, sledding, skating. I enjoyed the outdoors, teaching my little ones all these sports as they were growing up. Then there were the times when we went blue-berry picking, climbing the apple trees for those wonderful fruits, also, blackberry and raspberry picking. But the actual work of cleaning those berries and fruits, and harvesting the veggies in the gardens, seemed to be left up to me. Making the blueberry muffins and pies, freezing the veggies for the Winter, canning the tomatoes, and making pickles....then cleaning the messes in the kitchen....

and there was always vacuuming and laundry. Of course, the older children had their chores to do which was very helpful. My husband, Bill, worked his eight hours a day, but living, at first, 21 miles from work took almost an hour each way, so was quite weary when he would get home. There was always some repair work for him to do, whether on one of the cars, or a door hinge in the house, or cracked window pane, and certainly wood to be chopped for the stoves.

Yet, with all of this going on, there seemed to be something I was missing. Back in New Jersey Bill and I were very active in the church we were married in; teaching Sunday school, worship service, choir, Christmas pageants, etc. But! We were "social" drinkers, as were the church leaders, which, in my mind, I sometimes questioned. We attended parties and dances where alcoholic beverages were served, and yet, on Sundays we were attending church, as it was the thing to do, including participating in communion. After moving to the Catskills, it took us over a year before we were back in a church of the same religion as in New Jersey. Again, I was teaching Sunday school, singing in the choir, attending conferences, and became president of the ladies group. It never entered our minds why the Bible was hardly ever used in the pews. Even the Sunday school classes had instructional books to be taught from, rather than the Bible.

In the meantime, our oldest daughter, Nancy, who was about ten at the time, took advantage of "release time" at school. This was back in 1967. The educational system allowed "release time" once a week, for an hour. The children could stay in school or go to some church sponsored program. With our permission, Nancy opted for a church program called "Pioneer Girls". She always came home with cheerful reports of her time. One day she came off the school bus running up on the porch to tell me that she was "saved". She sounded rather excited, but as I was attending to her younger brother and sister, I just patted her shoulder and made a comment similar to, "that's nice, dear".

As I was searching for whatever was missing in my life, we were getting reports from family members through the summer, that my brother-in-law, Norman, back in New Jersey, had found 'religion'. He was becoming a 'holy-roller'. He had given up smoking, drinking, cussing, and was going to church regularly!! All of this was unbelievable to Bill and me. To add to that, one evening I was coming home from a church conference with the church leader and his wife. While he was driving, we started a conversation about the Bible stories I was teaching the beginners class on Sunday mornings. I am not sure just what I had asked that pastor, but he made a statement that, to this day, I cannot understand how he became a congregational leader. His statement was given as a question.

"Why, Kate, you don't really believe those fairy tales you are teaching, do you?!!"

What a thing to ask!!

"Why am I teaching those stories then? Adam and Eve? Noah and the Ark? David and Goliath?" I asked.

His answer was something to the effect, "those stories are just to teach good morals and rightful living." This answer was given as he was puffing on a cigarette!!

Wow!! No wonder the Bible isn't used in that type of a church.

Bill and I decided to take a long weekend to visit Norman and my sister, Mauvline, in New Jersey. We packed up the three younger children for the trip; the two older boys were old enough to stay home and take care of the farm and animals (15 and 17 at the time). They weren't too thrilled to go and visit relatives as most older teens feel. By the time we arrived in New Jersey, Norman had his pastor waiting there for us. The kids played with their cousins in the back yard, and after awhile, over coffee, Norman told us what happened to him. His girls were also members of a Pioneers Girls club, and had talked him into going to their church Easter service. It was an independent Baptist church, and the preacher had given a powerful message on 'salvation'. This was something neither Bill nor I had heard of in our 18 years of attending our religious church. Norman's pastor then explained God's plan of salvation. It was a bit much for me to take in. Later that evening, after supper, and putting the kids to bed, I went out on the back porch alone, and looking into the night sky at all of the stars, I searched for God and started talking to Him. It was my first time to have a general conversation with Him, rather than a stiff, meaningless prayer. Then I did what Norman's pastor suggested. I asked Jesus to forgive me of all my many sins, and that I was truly sorry. I then opened my heart and invited Him in. What a strange, but exciting feeling of relief, freedom, wonder, and peace! So, this is what salvation meant. I knew instantly I was saved from hell, and on my way to Heaven when the time would come. I later told Bill, but he wasn't ready to make the commitment. It was September 23, 1967, my birthday! It's the same date of my 'second' birthday. What a blessing!!

After getting home, I was excited of my 'happening', and could hardly wait to explain it at the next ladies meeting at church. When the time came, I started in. For some unknown reason, the church leader always attended the ladies meetings. Then, at that meeting he said, "Kate, we do not preach, or teach, salvation at this church."

What a blow!! Well, what to do?!? We continued going to that church half-heartedly. I continued teaching the "fairy tales", Bill and the kids good-naturedly continued to go along with my whims. But then, a few months later, my daughter, Nancy, told me the Pioneer Girls club was having a mother-daughter banquet and would like me to take her. It was at the Delhi Community Church, an independent Baptist church, coincidentally like the one my sister and brother-in-law were now attending. But was it really a coincidence? I told Nancy that of course we would go.

The banquet was lovely, and I finally met the Pioneer Girls leaders and other mothers. What friendly women! The church pastor's wife was the speaker. Everything she said was so enlightening to me as how mothers and daughters should depend on the Lord for all circumstances. She spoke directly from God's Holy Word, the Bible. Then and there, I made up my mind to attend that church. And again, Bill and the kids good-naturedly went along with this whim. A few weeks after we started to attend, the pastor and his wife invited Bill and me for dinner. That evening, in May, the pastor led Bill to the Lord to become saved!! Then, another few weeks after that, our oldest son, Bill, Jr., went forward at a church service and became saved. In August of 1968 the three of us were baptized by immersion at the Delhi Community Church. It felt so much more complete than when we were christened by sprinkling in the church we had attended previously.

My search was over. I found what was missing in my life. I realized we are all born with an empty spot in our hearts that can only be filled by God, Himself. Accepting Jesus as my Savior, that spot was filled. I continue to pray that I can convey this message to my friends and relatives. Some act like I did when Nancy first told me she had become saved and I brushed it off with "O, that's nice dear". If only people would realize how close they are to satan's grasp.

Living in the beautiful Catskill Mountains a verse from the Bible in the Old Testament book of Isaiah came to my mind just about every day I stepped outside....

"For ye shall go out with joy, and be led forth
    with peace;

The mountains and the hills shall break forth
    before you into singing,
And all the trees of the field shall clap their
    hands." Isaiah 55:12. (KJV)

Chapter 6

KITCHEN WINDOW THOUGHTS

The kitchen window is over the sink, and many times as I do the dishes I gaze out into the side lawn where I can view a small tree that was devastated by an ice storm several years before. The trunk of the tree is still standing, and it has a few dead branches poking up reaching toward the sky as if they were praying to be saved from the ice. Some of the side branches, even though dead, are able to hold a couple of bird feeders that I have hooked on to them. During the Spring I have seen various different birds come to the feeders. Red-winged blackbirds, robins, rufous-sided towhees, barn swallows, tree swallows, and, of course, the comical brown-headed cowbirds. The males are just that, comical. The feathers on their heads are brown to the nape of their necks. The rest of their bodies are black. Over all, when the sun glistens on them, their feathers are very sleek. When the males call, or whistle, they puff up their feathers - spread their tails - and almost fall over to release a high pitched squeak!

The females are a mousy brown color, similar to an oversized house sparrow. It is said that the female will take an egg out of the nest of some other bird and lay her own egg in the nest. Therefore, she never has the job of raising her own young. It is amazing then, how, later in the season, the cowbirds eventually flock together, even though they have been raised separately by some other type of bird. Naturally, our Creator has a purpose for all of this, even though we can't see it just now.

The cowbirds remind me of certain people. There are those of us who believe in God as our Creator, and also believe that His Son, Jesus Christ, is our Savior. But trying to spread this message we are stopped or discouraged on every side. Those who believe in the theory of evolution have, one by one, through the years, been taking the truths of God's Word out of the textbooks, the encyclopedias, the reference books, and any other materials they dare to, and lay the evolutionary eggs. There are those who go around all sleeked up and puffed up, who ruffle their feathers and almost fall off their pedestals as, with their high-pitched squeaks, they try to discredit, and twist around, the words of our Holy Bible. Then these same people get together in their own little groups, or flocks, and start bullying others, in fact, terrorizing others, if things don't go their way, or if they can't grab onto all they want....such as the cowbirds bullying other birds at the feeders to fill their own bellies. But, where do these flocks of cowbirds finally wind up? In the pastures following the cows - hence, their name - picking the leftover hayseed and corn out of the cow manure!

This, I believe, is what will happen to certain people. Our Creator will eventually have them wading in the mess, confusion, and misunderstanding, they themselves have caused by not believing in Creation.

Again, as I gaze out the window, and watch the birds at the feeders, I see the perky little chickadee, the cute red-poll, the junco, the weaver finch, (commonly called the English sparrow), and hear the beautiful melody of the song sparrow, and the sharp call of the blue jay. Then I begin to wonder why these species haven't inter-mingled in mating. Why haven't the chickadees developed brown streaks on their breasts, or the robin grown a crest on his head?? How can something like a one celled organism come out of the sea and eventually look like a bird; or another one celled organism turn into a sleek black panther; and another turn into the intricate form of a human being as the theory of evolution teaches? There is no rhyme or reason for this theory. Someone had to think up these things first. Someone had to decide on what creatures should have fins, and what creatures should have horns, and fur, and feathers, and beaks, and lips, and tentacles. To think that these things would grow automatically or accidentally, or form on creatures as time went on, is, in a simple word, dumb!

Creation by Someone is much easier to understand. It is impossible to understand evolution, but much more probable to conceive of Creation. The intricate details had to be thought of first, before even a worm could be created. Has anyone ever heard a praying mantis chirp like a katydid? Or an elephant crow like a rooster? Or a bullfrog chatter like a monkey? Can you imagine the surprise of a woman giving birth and instead of hearing her baby's first cry, it hoots like an owl? This is what evolution seems like to me....everything formed by chance. For thousands of years dogs have mated with dogs, eagles with eagles, sharks with sharks, and people with people. Nothing has been evolving that I know of. Maybe you would hear of something out of the ordinary, like a tiger with a lion, only because of the perverseness of man who has made them do so. Creation is much more beautiful to think of. A Creator has created dirt, water, grass, trees, tomatoes, bananas, elderberries, all sorts of vegetation! Then He created all kinds of fish and animals and birds, even tiny aphids for certain species of ants. To rule over all this, He created a man, and then a woman to be a man's 'help-meet'. When I think of myself as being created for that purpose, I can find my place on this earth. I know what I was created for, what I am expected to do, what someone expects of me. I am glad that I wasn't some one-celled thing, as it were, crawling up on the sands of time, wondering just what form or shape I would be, and what place I would come groveling to in this world.

Do you know what really puzzles me as I gaze out my window and watch a small flock of starlings join the other birds? Where did these one-celled little forms, or organisms, come from in the first place?!? Who created them?

Let me tell you of some lessons that have come to mind as I gazed out the kitchen window in the past. I have already mentioned the cowbird and its laziness in not making its own nest and expecting another bird to raise its young. It just sits by the feeder, too full to eat and too lazy to move out of the way for other birds to eat. Don't be like the cowbird. Laziness can affect you mentally, spiritually, and physically.

But, then, there is the little chickadee, which becomes so friendly that at times, I can open the window and put my hand out with a few seeds. It will perch on my hand and start pecking. Whether it eats from my hand or from the feeder its familiar notes of "chickadee-dee-dee-dee" will sound like "thank you-thank you" not only to me but to God. It makes me think of how we should be thankful for family, food, health, friends, the four seasons, and, of course, our Creator.

With its blue and white feathers, the blue jay is a bright and beautiful bird. The problem with this bird is that he is greedy and noisy, and picks on the smaller birds — all bad habits. How many of us keep ourselves looking good on the outside but harbor these bad habits on the inside and ruin our inner looks? This is where we need help from God to get rid of bad habits. Ask Him to clean our hearts - our inner being.

A very choosy bird is the nuthatch. It picks its seeds very carefully, eating only certain kinds. It is a reminder to us to be careful of what we eat, especially when snacking on salty or sweet things between meals; especially, also, what we eat for our meals. Everyone's favorite seems to be the beautiful red cardinal. Both, male and female, are equally responsible in caring for their young. If, for some reason, they lose their own offspring, they will start feeding other cardinals babies. Are we being fed by others? Not just with food, but with love, tender care, ideas, the Word of God? Do we pay attention when the preacher is preaching to us, or when being taught a lesson in Sunday School? All of us should go to a church where there is Sunday School for young and old alike.

The weaver finch is called the English sparrow. It looks and acts like a sparrow. You really can't tell the difference. I sometimes wonder if people can tell that I am a Christian. Do I act like someone who loves, and has the love of, God? Do I push my way through the grocery stores? Or do I let someone go before me through the checkout line if there is a crying baby in their cart, or if an elderly person only has one or two things in a basket? Do I blow my car horn if the driver ahead of me doesn't take off as soon as the light turns green? Do you act like a good Christian but know in your heart that you really aren't one? I pray that you talk to the Lord about that.

The evening grosbeak, with its pretty colors of black, white, and yellow likes to stay with its own kind in a flock. It doesn't welcome other kinds of birds. This is something we have to be careful about. When we meet someone who acts, thinks, or looks different, do we hesitate to invite him or her to our church? We must remember that God's love is for everyone.

The song sparrow is not very big or colorful, but it sings its beautiful song, loud and clear. If we have a special gift such as singing or the talent of playing an instrument, we should not keep it to ourselves. We should use it to give praise to our Lord, our Creator.

Being a Sunday School teacher at one time, these thoughts and lessons sound like something to be taught to children perhaps, but I think we can all use these lessons from the birds. So many lessons come to me as I gaze out the kitchen window while doing the dishes, making this household chore a real delight. The move to the Catskill Mountains has been so rewarding to me that it seems I learn something every day.

Chapter 7

GETTING BACK TO BREAD MAKING

I wrote this article back in 1972 when we were living in the first farm we bought. So, bear with me as I reminisce back to that time. But, it is in the present tense.

Today I decided to make bread. That's right! Real homemade bread! It was something I had gotten away from since I had gone out to work these past four years. But now I am at home again after quitting my job a few months ago. Our older two boys have flown out of the nest. They are in the military. The three younger children are still in school, but I felt I was needed at home for when they are here. I just saw them onto the school bus at 7:45 A.M. and they won't be back till 3:45 P.M. I have plenty of time to bake.

It's a beautiful spring day - everything turning green, but there is a steady rain coming down.

Becoming a bird-watcher, I've been at the front door for fifteen minutes watching the birds as they fly out onto the lawn for the couple of cups of birdseed I had thrown out there (which I do every morning). There are six spruce trees surrounding the lawn, each within a stone's throw from the front porch. There are about two dozen grackles building nests in the tops of these trees, which hover over our 100 year old 'split-level', three story, farmhouse. There are starlings nesting at the back of the house behind the chimney, which has loosened from the outside wall of the house. The robins haven't started their nests as yet, but most build theirs in the old apple orchard along the front driveway.

There is also a huge eastern cottonwood tree near the spruce trees that must have been planted when the house was built. I know there was another one nearby at one time before we bought this place, which was struck by lightning, and the trunk was left to rot, but finally sawn down. I often think of what could happen if the remaining one was hit by lightning. Why, even just one of it's large branches would be enough to come crashing through the roof. Sometimes when a fierce storm wakes me up at night I watch out the bedroom window as the lightning flashes, and I can see the outline of the huge trunk and branches and think how terribly much I would miss that tree if it were knocked down. I wouldn't be the only one to miss it. I couldn't begin to count how many chickadees and blue-jays have perched in that tree waiting for their morning handout during the winter. Through the worst winter days they are the only visitors we have for days at a time. An occasional nut-hatch would also brave the elements. So, when spring finally arrives - not March 21 as the calendar indicates - but around now, the first week of May, it becomes a thrill to watch for the birds to return. So far today, I have seen the grackles, starlings, robins, chickadees, the bothersome brown-headed cowbirds, the pretty white-throated sparrows, a chipping sparrow, and a song sparrow, and the misnamed English sparrow. I guess the barn and tree swallows have decided to stay up in the barn out of the rain.

Now, after 20 or 25 minutes of bird watching, I'm having a cup of tea and found that the last crust of bread was toasted for one of the children's breakfast. I really didn't need a piece of toast anyway, since I've gained some weight like the proverbial contented cow. Then, I thought that means a trip to the corner grocery store sometime today - which seems unnecessary, since the store is not just around the corner in the country, it's three miles away!! So, I gazed up at my cook-book shelf and realized how foolish I was - forty cents for a loaf of bread, when in one of my cook-books was a great recipe called "Perfect White Bread" which makes six loaves that would cost me about fourteen cents a loaf, praise the Lord! I have all the ingredients, and I would make it more nutritious because there would be no additives. I can also sneak in some whole-wheat flour fortified with brewer's yeast that I had bought from an organic company. Yes, I am gradually becoming a natural food 'nut'!

As I am now making the batter and kneading it, I read a poem that was printed on the opposite page from the recipe. I had read it before but it never struck me as interesting. But, today, what with the country filled with women talking about liberation and equal rights, it hit me! This poem made me realize that if women opened their hearts, not only their eyes, they would realize that they have been liberated since time began - and that they have not only been equal, but highly respected and honored more than men.

Let me quote this poem found in the book, "Favorite Breads From Rose Lane Farms".

"I Am Many Women"

When sky and street merge in sullen grayness
    and black trees stir in sleep,
My stove becomes a hearth.
I am many women who have looked at rain
    through a flap of hide,
From a hand hewn door, and felt secure
    against a threatening world,
Blessed within warm walls and sheltering
    roof.
Hands deep in flour, powdered grain from a
    million fields,
Garnered in sweating sunlight.
I am many women who have kneaded resil-
    ient dough with strong hands....
Brown, red, yellow, and white hands.
Folding and stretching, shaping smoothly
    contoured loaves
Rich with the smell of yeast.

(Bread is nothing so much as bread, sacred in
 its own identity.)
The sky trades snow for night,
And the scent of baking loaves is calm bene-
 diction for my home.
I am many women who have taken bread
 from an oven,
And breaking it....
Felt consecrated.
Anon.

Chapter 8

THE MYSTERIOUS MONARCH

It was in early September, as I would sit outside and enjoy the scenery, and fall flowers, and changing colors of the trees, that I began to notice a migration of a different sort. Not of birds or geese, but a beautiful butterfly. Every five or ten minutes I would notice one heading south. Not in flocks, but singly. Eventually I checked a couple of encyclopedia and put together this interesting story. Do you like mysteries? Do you ever wonder why some things are so simple, and yet, other things are so mysterious? With all of His creations, God, at times, has given us creatures that we want to study about. Sometimes, the more we study about them, the more mysterious they are!

One of God's creatures that is full of mystery is the monarch butterfly. Did you know that this butterfly migrates? That is, it flies south for the winter, just as robins or Canada geese do. Some of them migrate over 2,000 miles down the map of North America. They flutter with their black and orange wings from Canada down through the New England states to Florida; or down through the mid-western states like Michigan, or Wisconsin, to Texas; or from Canada down through the states of Washington and Oregon to southern California and into Mexico.

One by one during the autumn days they leave the fields and meadows where milkweed is abundant. Then, in a drifting movement, they instinctively hold their southerly course for days and weeks while the trees around them change from northern spruce to apple to cypress and the moss-hung live oaks of the Gulf Coast or the palms and orange groves of the Florida peninsula.

Monarchs drift down the Long Island shore crossing the New York Bay in their direct southerly flight and sometimes come to rest in southern New Jersey before moving on. Others move south over the mountains in Pennsylvania. Still others flutter over the flatlands of Ohio, or cross the wild Au Sable River in northern Michigan and migrate down over the Mississippi River. They move along the mountains of Nevada and even cross the shimmering desert of the salt flats in Utah. Those in the west fly down the Pacific coast past the Douglas firs and over the great redwoods drifting toward their winter home at Pacific Grove in California.

The monarch butterfly's annual movement receives the most attention at Pacific Grove, a community overlooking Monterey Bay on the California coast. It is one of the few insect sanctuaries in the world. Sometimes, as many as two million butterflies spend the winter here, concentrating in an area of only a few acres. In masses they cling to the branches and needles of the pines there. With wings closed, they pack together like gray-brown leaves. For days at a time they cling in the same spot. They are not really hibernating, they are only semi-dormant. One of the mysteries of the monarch is how can it return instinctively to those very same pines year after year. Its life cycle is too short; therefore the monarch never makes the fall migration a second time. It returns instinctively, without leaders.

The monarch is nicknamed the milkweed butterfly. It begins its life in a jewel-like, pointed pale green egg, that is usually laid close to one of the ribs on the underside of a milkweed leaf. In about five days the caterpillar that hatches from the egg is only about one eighth of an inch long. It devours its egg shell then is hungry for only one food -the juicy tissues of the milkweed plant. When it reaches full size, it is a striking caterpillar with bands of black and white and yellow. In about three weeks it attaches itself by its tail, which has a pair of hooked legs, to a bit of silk that it places on a twig. Then it hangs upside down with its head curved upward. The larval skin splits open from the bottom up and is shed completely. Then the creature turns into a pupa, or, chrysalis, of a beautiful waxy green color with spots of gold.

In nine to fifteen days the chrysalis splits open and the adult butterfly emerges. Another of God's mysteries presented to us. The monarch has large compound eyes that have hundreds of facets, and are attached to a freely moving head. The front and rear wings (about two inches long) are well developed and covered with tiny scales. This butterfly is a strong flier. It flaps and glides in calm and moderate winds, but facing a stiff breeze, it beats its wings steadily and can force its way ahead into winds that are strong enough to set the branches of small trees tossing.

The monarch was originally found only in North and South America. Its range, in all forms, extends from Nova Scotia and British Columbia in Canada, to Argentina. There may be as many as three or four generations in one season. It is usually the last generation that forms the bulk of those that migrate. Sometimes they gather in small groups or loose flocks when their southward movement begins. Usually though, they go alone but stay close together without a leader. Year after year they seem to come to the same resting place as their ancestors did. One hundred monarchs were once counted clinging on a small branch in Long Island.

One of the mysterious or puzzling things about the millions of monarchs that make the long journey southward is that only a very few of them come north in the spring -and they come singly. They are weatherworn and faded and go almost un-noticed. Are the northern areas repopulated by just the few returning migrants or by a new generation of butterflies? Do the few that return stop part way along the map and produce a new generation that, in turn, travels instinctively northward -something like a relay race? Some scientists believe that the monarchs who reach the

northern limits are perhaps a second or third generation of the ones that left the southern migration range.
So many mysteries remain obscure of this familiar,
and beautiful, black-and-orange insect.

Another puzzling thing is that, when headed
south, the migrating monarch rises over obstruc-
tions such as buildings or clumps of bushes or trees,
instead of going around them. They seem set on a
compass course, but what compass do they use? It
seems that we sometimes take things for granted, like
the many species of butterflies. It is when we start to
observe them singly, and study them, that we realize
God has created beautiful and wondrous creatures.
He has a purpose for each of His creations, perhaps
for nothing more than His pleasure, and for ours; like
the beautiful, mysterious Monarch butterfly.

Chapter 9

BOATING IN THE CATSKILLS

When living in New Jersey, Bill and I enjoyed going to the various salt-water rivers and bays, even the ocean, to do some fishing. In fact, some of our dates before we were married were fishing dates. I had to learn how to put worms and live shiners on the hooks, and in turn, take the fish that I caught off the hooks. We also enjoyed eating any of the seafood we caught.

Moving up to the Catskills, we missed those fishing trips. Two or three times a year we did go back to New Jersey to fish. Our kids were getting old enough to enjoy it also. Many times we would come back to the mountains with one or two hundred good-sized fish - blue fish, weak fish, flounder, porgies, mackerel, - whatever was in season. Filling up our freezers with enough to last the winter, we then gave the rest away to our neighbors.

Living on the proverbial 'shoe-string', we just could not afford a decent boat. After a few years we found a boat for sale, cheap, near the East Sidney Dam State Park. This was a very accommodating park with a large lake, about forty miles from where we were living. Oh, my, did this boat need a lot of repair!! A trailer went with it, so we were able to tow it back to Bovina. Finally, getting it all workable, including the outboard engine, it was ready. The boat had no roof, just a windshield in the front, with enough room for about six people to fit in comfortably.

Taking it back over to East Sidney Dam, we tested it out. It ran like a charm. We were excited to think we could take the kids, (and by now, grand-kids), out boating and fishing. What fun we had when we would bring it to East Sidney for family picnics. We'd also bring it over for church Sunday School picnics. Several other families would have their boats and all the kids, including the grown-up kids, enjoyed a turn on the water. A few times we'd have water skis that were a highlight of the fun. There were also times we'd take the boat out on the Otsego Lake in Cooperstown.

There was one time, though, (I barely remember it), we were at East Sidney having a family picnic. This time the kids enjoyed being towed on old truck tubes. Bill, and our son-in-law, George, went in the boat with some kids for a ride. After a while it seemed they were gone for some time. Being that there were some bends in the long lake, we couldn't see them. We did know that the engine was having fits at times, so we kept hoping they weren't in trouble. Apparently they were!! It had given out! Eventually we saw the boat coming back around the bend rather slowly - George in the front, paddling with what looked like a 2 x 4 about 6 ft. long. Bill was steering and paddling, also with a piece of lumber. That's right! We had no oars on the boat! Come to think of it, we only had one back home. It was quite a sight, though, and I was so glad I had brought my camera to take a shot of that memory. Guess what we received as Christmas presents that year from our daughter and her husband?! Uh-huh!! Right! A pair of oars, etched with His and Hers on them.

After many repairs and overhauls, and paint, Bill eventually became brave enough to tow the boat all the way to New Jersey. We would leave about two or three in the morning, rattling down the N.Y. State Thruway, and then the N.J. State Parkway, in our old Chevy Blazer, pulling the boat on the trailer, (I would secretly keep praying we'd get to our destination without any incident), and arrive at Raritan Bay around 6 or 7 A.M. Bringing coolers filled with drinks and sandwiches, etc., we'd fish until 3 or 4 in the afternoon, filling the coolers with fish as we emptied out our lunches. Depending on how many of us came to fish, we usually had a nice catch to bring home. The trip home was always tiring, but we made it. What fun it was - although the smell was something else - fishy - sweaty - and it seemed no matter what skin protection we had, we would be burned a bright red from the sun!

One time our older sons, Bill and Ed, and a grand-son, Noel, took the boat to New Jersey. I can't remember the whole story, but we received a phone call from them in the afternoon...our oldest wanted to talk to Dad. Oh, oh!

"What's the problem?" Dad asked. We just knew there had to be a problem!!

"You won't believe this," Bill, Jr. said, "But.... we lost the boat trailer!"

"The boat trailer! No, I can't believe it! Tell it to me, slowly, please!"

Bill, Jr. began to explain, something like, "We were pulling the boat up out of the water, and had pulled the plug out of it to drain, when all of a sudden the chain snapped, and came loose from the truck! It rolled back down the ramp into the water, and we realized the water was coming into the boat. By the time we swam into the water and released the boat and put the plug back in, the trailer sank!! There is so much mud and muck where the trailer went down we can't even feel it with the oars. It must be buried!!"

"Do you have the boat tethered?" Dad asked, in a surprisingly calm voice. "Is it O.K.? Are the three of you O.K.?"

"Yes, it's tied to a dock. Yes."

"Here's what you are going to have to do," Bill (Dad) told him. "YOU are going to call my nephew, Mark, tell him your dilemma, and then tell him to call me."

"Dad, can't you call him? We are pretty much embarrassed!"

"No."

Mark lived in the area and we knew he would get quite a kick out of the story. He has a boat and trailer and we knew he had friends in the boat yards. We eventually heard from Mark who said (as he was chuckling) he would be helping the boys out by borrowing a trailer and towing the boat to his place in Carteret near where we used to live. We told him we'd be there as soon as possible. Arriving in the evening, we visited Bill's sister who obligingly put us all up for the night. The boys sleeping on the floor!! In the morning we all had quite a chuckle about the whole incident, with Bill and Ed taking the brunt of the flack, good-naturedly.

But, then came the question as how to get the boat home, with no trailer?! We couldn't afford to buy one, and we had to take the one that was loaned back to the boat yard. Bill and I decided that the boat was not in much of a shape any more. Being that Carteret was on the river separating it from Staten Island, the Boy Scouts had a unit called the Sea Scouts there. Bill called them and asked if they could use the boat, even if just to learn how to repair it and navigate it. The Scout leader was very appreciative with the idea, so Bill and our sons and Mark towed it to the river. Making sure it was staying afloat, Mark then returned the trailer.

It was quite an event for all of us! My sons laugh about it now. We can't remember what happened to the fish, or even if there was any fish caught! Eventually, we did buy another boat, again a second hand one. Believe it or not, Bill towed it all the way to Florida when we became 'sno-birds', enjoying Lake Weir and the Ocklawaha River, in beautiful Marion County.

Chapter 10

GLOOMY MONDAY
MORNING

The trend of the morning actually started the night before. And, since this happened quite a while back, I can't remember if it really was a Monday. Friend husband and I both were working the evening shift of 3:P.M. to 11:P.M. But he worked 4 miles from home at the state school for delinquent boys, and I worked 16 miles away as an aide at a county nursing home for the infirmed and the aged. I really got off from work at 11:15, so hubby is home about a half hour before me.

Therefore, that night when I arrived home, he had my usual cup of tea ready, and we watched the end of the best of Donahue on T.V. (remember him??), It had something to do with people laid off in the Chicago area, who were upset because of the Reaganomics situation. They were telling of their jobs where they made $10 to $15 an hour. $40 to

$50 thousand a year!! We turned it off and discussed the situation a bit. We felt we were happy up here in the rural mountains of the Catskills making our combined pay of $25,000. We had a nice big warm home, two cars, 15 acres; the five 'kids' had all flown from the proverbial nest....What more did we need?

As we were getting ready for bed, hubby said, "By the way, I brought up kindling wood and logs for you to start the fire in the morning. You won't have to go down in the cellar when you wake up."

"Thank you, dear!!"

It was really my own fault that I had this habit of getting up early in the morning to start the coffee going. But, now we had a gas stove with a connecting wood burning unit also, to beat the rising oil prices. We had renovated the kitchen and dining room by tearing out the wall between the rooms, putting up barn beams on the ceiling and barn wood around the lower half of the walls in the dining area. A chimney was made on the outside wall for the wood burning unit, and weathered brick on the wall behind this stove. (Tried to run the brick around the kitchen cabinets, but ran out of funds.) We painted the top half of the walls a Dutch blue since we were of Dutch descent. (but ran out of funds to buy linoleum for the floors).

Getting back to that morning, I at least wouldn't have to run down into the cold cellar for an armload of wood and get sawdust all over my warm, fuzzy bathrobe. It would be a pleasure when I got up around 8:A.M. I usually turn up the thermostat for the oil furnace just enough to take the chill out of the air as I started the wood fire.

But!! That morning it was 7:A.M. when something woke me up! What was that different noise?! Come on, brain waves, wake up! What do I hear?? Aha! It was the water pump! We didn't have city or village running water. Ours came from a well out in the back lawn and pumped in. The pump! Continuously running. Oh, no!! What's the sense of waking up dear husband?! It would take a half hour to register with him. So, on went the slippers and bathrobe and I'm going down into the cold cellar any way. Water running over half the floor. It happened! The hot water heater had a tiny leak in it for the past year and it turned into a big hole, like a water faucet! So, I turned off the pump, went back upstairs to tell friend husband, who, in turn said, "Did you think of turning off the water pump?"

I said, "Yes."

He said, "O.K."....turned over and went back to sleep!!

So, I stayed awake. There was just enough water left in the teakettle to heat for a cup of tea. The sun was just coming up, and out in the field were birds. They must be the red-winged blackbirds, and it's their first day up from the south. God sent me some consolation. Finding my binoculars, I started to watch them and did pick out a few red-wings, but, then, the binoculars started to steam up. The vacuum seal around the lens was leaking and fogged up just when things came into focus! What a bummer! Couldn't even ease my mind by bird watching.

With a few so-called 'crocodile' tears, I went into the bedroom and bounced onto the bed boo-hooing, and feeling sorry for myself. The big teddy-bear husband put his warm arms around me and let me sob out my woes of the binoculars, the water tank, and especially my wet slippers and fuzzy bathrobe.

His next remark was, "But did you start the fire in the wood-burning stove in the kitchen? After all, I brought up that nice dry wood for you last night!!"

After I pounded him on the back a few times with the wet slippers, we finally went out into the warm kitchen, had some hot milk, and seriously discussed our dilemma. Fortunately, we had a sump pump in the cellar floor, which was draining the water. A neighbor plumber was able to get us a new water tank and installed it that morning! Remember, that was over 25 years ago! Try to get that kind of help now.

That afternoon, as we were getting ready to go to work, we praised the Lord for the way He handled things. We knew that sooner or later we had to get a new water heater. God arranged for the bigger leak 'sooner' in the morning while we were yet home. If it happened 'later' after we left for work, the cellar floor would have been flooded, perhaps enough to ruin the oil furnace. It might have been too much for the sump pump to handle. And! It could have run the well dry. We have a great God! Thank you, Lord.

That was part of life in Catskill Country!!

Chapter 11

IRVING

There were always wonderful little surprises living in Catskill country. The flora and fauna amazed me every time I went for a walk whether in the fields or the woods. I usually would see something new and different, but there was a time I found something right at my back door. It was during the winter when I brought in an armful of logs for our fireplace. A piece of bark broke away from one of the logs, and then I saw it!!

On the bare wood was this black thing, all curled up. Yukk!! Finding an empty jar, I gently prodded the thing into it with a stick. Its body slowly uncurled and I realized it was a salamander. It was shiny black except for a double row of yellow spots down its back, approximately seven inches long. It looked up at me with large black eyes as if to say, "Why have you disturbed me? I have just settled down for a long winter's nap!" For some unknown reason, I named it Irving.

After tending to the fireplace, I watched as Irving curled back up again in the jar. Then I checked my bookshelves for articles on salamanders. I learned that the yellow-spotted black salamander is a land dwelling amphibian that likes warm, moist places. It cannot be exposed to air for very long without replacing the water in its body, yet it cannot drink or absorb moisture from the air. Therefore, it takes in water through the skin. So, when necessary, the amphibian backs into wet sand or mud and flattens its body on the moist surface to absorb water. Sometimes it sits or swims in a puddle or a pool. The salamander prefers a dark place to hide and cannot make noises; therefore, it escapes many daytime predators. At night it must be careful of skunks, bobcats, coyotes, and raccoons, which are found in most of the Catskills. It likes to hibernate during the winter and curls up under logs, stones, piles of leaves, and under loose bark of dead trees and logs, where I found Irving.

With that knowledge, I made a home for him in a large globe type terrarium that I had plants in. I added large shells, some small stones, and a few pieces of bark for him to hide under. I used a small bowl for his 'soaking' pool and placed it in the soil that I built up to the brim. This was kept filled with fresh water. Irving liked worms, slugs, grubs, and all sorts of insects, as long as they were alive, but his favorite was worms. During the winter it was hard to find any live food for him and there were days that he went hungry. But, then he would crawl under a shell or piece of bark and hibernate....or was he just sulking? Once in a while a stray fly would happen by and someone would catch it and put it in the terrarium. As it crawled on the shells or plants, Irving would stalk it until he was able to snap his mouth around it, and then he'd creep around looking for more.

What fun it was for my grandchildren to feed him. They would dangle a worm in front of him and tease him a bit, until he ferociously jumped at it. With that, the grandchild holding the worm would drop it, thinking his finger would be bitten off. Irving was always a source of conversation. Many times I was asked, "Why do you keep such an ugly thing as that?" "How can you touch the worms that you feed to him?" "Is he dangerous to the children?" "Is he poisonous?" "Aren't you afraid that he will bite?" I could never see any teeth in Irv's mouth. The children loved to watch him, and some were even brave enough to hold him.

After Irving lived in the terrarium for over five years, I decided to give it a good cleaning and change the plant arrangement. It was summer, so I was able to do the job out on the patio, on the picnic table. I put Irv in a tall coffee can with some leaves and grass to keep him cool and to hide under. I had gone inside several minutes to wash the bowl, and then came back outside. When it was time to put Irving back in the clean terrarium, he was gone!! He absolutely vanished. He wasn't in the can, or on the picnic table, or on the patio, or in the flower gardens along the side of the patio. Surely I would be able to see those yellow spots of his if he was scampering down the driveway! To no avail. Irving was not to be found anywhere. I felt a sadness….a disappointment. Why did I go inside those few minutes without him? Why didn't I put the lid on the can?

Every day while working in the gardens or mowing the lawn, or when I hung out laundry, I would look for that little creature with the yellow spots. I knew he would find enough worms and grubs to eat, and there was plenty of water, but I wondered if he remembered enough to protect himself from his enemies. The articles I had read on amphibians said that salamanders lived in the wild for at least two or three years, and some had lived in captivity for thirty years. I have no idea how old Irving was when I found him, but I had him for over five years. Also, the average length of a yellow-spotted salamander is seven inches. Irving had grown to nine inches long.

I suppose some people who live or visit in the Catskills think this is a mundane thing to write about, but it is the little things in life that are amusing, educational, and interesting. The Catskills were a good place to take time to smell the flowers, talk to chickadees, listen to the rustling leaves, and watch a salamander. I still wonder about Irving. I wonder if he survived without food at times. I wonder about the way water got into his body. I wonder how he was able to live in that terrarium all those years. One of the things I wonder the most about; his name, Irving. Perhaps I should have called that salamander…. Alice!!!!

CHAPTER 12

EASTER VACATION
OF 1968

Living in a wonderful vacation area of the Catskill Mountains, with its changing seasons, and fun all year round - (fun, that is, for the kids, much work for all of us to keep the place going..) - we began to realize that there are other places to go to, and sights to see. Yes, we did visit friends and relatives back in New Jersey; and, yes, while visiting, there were times we were able to go to the beaches to swim or fish. But, when our oldest boy, Bill, Jr., was planning to enlist in the Coast Guard after he graduated high school, we realized, also, that we never had a real vacation together as a family.

When I said to Bill, Sr., "We should, somehow, take the time and find the money to go away. Let's take the kids for a trip."

It surprised me when he said, "I think that's a great idea! But, financially, we've got to cut it tight!"

The five children were all for it, even the two teen-aged boys - Bill and Ed. They agreed to help save 'pennies' by donating once in a while from whatever jobs they could find helping the near-by farmers. The younger three would save from their allowances. On special occasions that we took to go out to eat before we went shopping, we would go to fast food places or a cheap diner. Bill and I would for-go desserts. We also started to buy extra groceries; canned soups, veggies, tuna, other canned meats, boxed cereals, jello, puddings, jars of fruits, applesauce; anything we could pack that would 'keep', for our two week trip. We planned on finding motels with kitchenettes where we could have meals without going out to restaurants.

My Mom had sent me a booklet, which told of places to visit for free. It was very useful. I kept pouring over it and picked out a few places I knew the kids would like - young and old. Do they have such books any more with free places to go? I don't know, but back then it was certainly handy.

We decided that the best time for this trip was Easter week, leaving Thursday, April 11. Asking the principal of the school for permission for the days before Easter vacation week, he was very accommodating in saying, "It's fine, providing they do assigned home-work from their teachers; but, most of all, the children should write some reports on what they saw and did." A few schoolbooks, pads and pencils were packed in the kids' bags, and believe it or not, they didn't mind at all.

Of all things, the day we were packing the car and getting ready to leave, our oldest daughter, Nancy, eleven at the time, started crying. Between her sobs, she cried, "I smashed my thumb in the car door!!" I knew that had to be quite painful for her the first few days. I wrapped her thumb the best that I could.

After stowing the groceries and drinks in the back of the station wagon, and tying down the luggage on the roof, the kids all got in with their own little 'goodie' bags, and we headed south on the New York Thruway.... destination, Virginia Beach, by way of Long Island. A half hour on the Thruway and a rear tire blew out!! Needless to say, boxes and coolers had to be removed since the spare tire was in the well under the floorboard. Bill and I kept hoping the spare would be O.K. till we arrived in Long Island. We could get it fixed (or buy a new tire) when we stopped at a motel. We also had some friends we would be visiting in Oakdale. They were very helpful with getting the tire fixed.

The younger kids were amazed as we traveled over the George Washington Bridge. I rather enjoyed it myself. They were also amazed at all of the traffic. They hadn't experienced New York City traffic since growing up in the country.

Bill and Ed enjoyed meeting our friends in Long Island since they found out they had two teen-aged daughters. The next day, Friday, we invited the girls to come with us as we had planned on visiting and picnicking at the Bayard Cutting Arboretum in Great River, Long Island. Their parents were working that day. It was a bit early for the Spring flowers to be blooming, but the Arboretum was still beautiful to hike on the trails through this state park. The kids had brought balls to toss, so the nine of us enjoyed the exercise, running and catching, and just having fun. We spent some time in the evening with our friends and then went to the motel to collapse! At least, Bill and I did!

Saturday, the 13th, we left Oakdale with the sun shining brightly as we traveled on the Southern State Parkway, passing Coney Island (which was rapidly changing - for the worst - at that time). Driving over the Verrazano - Narrows Bridge, another marvelous bridge - we came to Staten Island. We stretched our legs by visiting and walking through the "biggest little zoo on Earth" in Barrett Park, called the Staten Island Zoo. This was a great place to visit with no admission fee!! Is this zoo still there? I don't know since we've never been back.

Another bridge then took us into New Jersey where we visited with relatives the rest of the day, staying with them Saturday and Sunday nights. Easter morning we attended the church where Bill and I were married in 1948. WOW! Was it that long ago?!?

Early Monday morning we headed south toward Cape May, N.J. Finding a nice motel in North Wildwood we unpacked our 'stuff'. Driving to the Stone Harbor Bird Sanctuary, we saw many species of herons and other birds. I'm not sure, but it even seemed that the older boys were enjoying that park. Eventually, we went beach combing along the ocean. Children of any age enjoy running along the beach, and seeing what they can find....including Bill and me.

The next morning, April 16, we drove through the lovely Victorian village of Cape May, stopping at Cape May Point where there was a lighthouse, but it was closed. After some beach-combing we drove a bit further and came to a pretty little lake and fed ducks and geese and pigeons; eating our 'brunch' at a picnic table nearby. At Cape May Inlet the boys found their fishing poles and caught a couple of nice flounder, while the younger kids found some nice big shells to take home. As we looked across the river which flowed into the inlet, we saw the Coast Guard Station where Bill, Jr. was to train when he leaves us in October. We could see some of the men practicing with fire-fighting equipment. Also, a Coast Guard cutter went out toward the Atlantic Ocean. It gave me a proud feeling, but, yet, a feeling of apprehension.

An hour later we came to another exciting part of the trip. We drove onto the Cape May Ferry to cross the mouth of Delaware Bay at the Atlantic Ocean, going to Lewes, Delaware. This was a new experience for all of the kids. The younger ones couldn't believe so many cars could fit onto a boat!! It could carry 1200 passengers and 124 cars on any given day. The 16.3 mile trip takes almost 70 minutes.

When the ferry started, 7-year-old Tommy was holding his stomach and said, "It feels as if there are a lot of little fishes swimming in my stomach!"

After we all got out of the car, he soon forgot his queasy stomach as we began to walk each deck and watched other boats out on the water. Then, of course, they enjoyed buying snacks and drinks at the food bar.

From Lewes we traveled along Ocean Drive and stopped at Indian River Bay to do some fishing and play in the sand. Have you come to the conclusion that our older boys and their father enjoy fishing? Then, a bit further south, just past Ocean City, Maryland, we came to a motel called Ebb Tide, with a kitchenette. Being April 16th, it was Bill, Sr.'s birthday. We celebrated supper with a fish fry from all that was caught. We had purchased fresh vegetables and also cup-cakes to put candles in.

Bill said, "This is one of my favorite birthdays!!" He became 40 years old.

Heading south once more on Rte. 13 on Wednesday, we were on our way to Wallops Island, Virginia. We had written ahead for a 1:30 P.M. reservation to take a tour of the NASA station there. This tour was also a 'freebie'. I should say, it was, back in 1968. Luckily, we were the only ones scheduled for that time of day. A very big and nice Sergeant guided us around in a base van. Going first to the Range Control Station, we watched men controlling everything by push-button instruments as they watched on T.V. screens the rockets being shot off their pads seven miles away. We were then taken through a building that housed many displays of space rockets and satellites - including a life-sized replica of a two-man satellite.

Getting back into the base vehicle, the Sergeant drove us over to the launch site in time to see two small rockets being shot off. In the meantime, Nancy had a large blood blister develop on the thumb she had caught in the car door. I had been changing the dressing every day, but she must have taken it off that morning for some reason that I wasn't aware of. The blister broke at the launch site, blood spattering all over her clothes and into the vehicle! The Sergeant very calmly took her into a building right there, (I wasn't allowed), fortunately it housed a first aid station. Nancy had the privilege of having a nurse clean and dress her wound.

The tour took about 2 and ½ hours. Our guide admitted, though, that the day before, he had a group of 90 fifth graders (which was a little too much) to which he couldn't explain in detail everything that was going on because of all the noise and fidgeting. That day the tour was over in less than two hours. He was more at ease and rather leisurely with our family of seven. It was very interesting to our whole family, even the girls. This tour was especially worthwhile for any students interested in the aeronautics field.

Just a bit east of Wallops Island, we went over a bridge that crossed Chincoteague Bay and Channel to the island of Chincoteague. The girls were excited with the thought of seeing wild ponies and horses reportedly living on this island. We did see some grazing in swamps and meadows, but at a distance. We found a nice, cozy bungalow to stay in, but were warned we may have some little visitors (mice) since it was too early for the tourist season, and it hadn't been cleaned as well as it should be. We took it any way, being used to mice in our old farmhouse back home.

Thursday morning we woke up to a beautiful sunrise. After some breakfast, we drove over to Assateague Island, which is a natural preserve for wildlife, especially the ponies and horses. The area just before the sand dunes were being developed for public use with the placement of picnic tables, grills, and rest rooms. Otherwise, it was, and still is, a beautiful, pristine, clean beach of many miles. The kids would have loved to go in swimming, but being April, the water was quite cold, even for just their feet. In fact, we all needed jackets just to stroll on the beach and collect a few shells. After a walk through some of the nature trails we left the ponies and horses in Assateague and Chincoteague.

A little disappointed, Nancy exclaimed, "They aren't wild! They are all behind fences, just like on a farm!!"

But the girls did get books about the wild horses, and the boys bought various souvenirs.

Thursday afternoon we drove down the Delmarva Peninsula and crossed over the now famous Chesapeake Bay Bridge Tunnel, one of my favorite bridges. A beautiful drive of 17 1/2 miles across the Chesapeake Bay, consisting of two tunnels, each about a mile long. The kids were really amazed! After going through the second tunnel, which goes under the Thimble Shoal channel, we came out by the Sea Gull fishing pier. Naturally, we all wanted to stop and walk the long pier. There was also a nice restaurant; we were quite hungry and splurged on a very late lunch. It was a wonderful place to sit and eat as we watched the fishing boats and large tankers go over the water we had just been under. We could also see people fishing along the pier. As we were leaving some more souvenirs were purchased.

Continuing our southerly route, we arrived at Virginia Beach. It was quite crowded with students on Easter vacation (now called Spring break). The boardwalk, with its many amusements and fairly new hotels, looked a bit too expensive for us, and we had to explain that problem to the kids, much to their chagrin! Our funds were half gone and it was time to turn the car around. Traveling back we saw the Fort Story and Fort Henry lighthouses which seemed to be good places to visit, and the older kids could report on the history of them for school. Again, we were dismayed since both places were closed for repairs. We then came to the Seashore State Park and decided to hike on some of the trails, especially on the Bald Cypress Nature Trail. It was quite interesting since we came upon many trees and shrubs that were quite different from what we were used to in the Catskills. Most amazing to the kids was to see the Spanish moss hanging from the trees. The wildlife, especially the birds, were in abundance - also different from the northern birds.

Taking the highway back toward the Bay Bridge Tunnel, we came to Lynnhaven Inlet and found a nice motel on the bay beach, just east of the inlet. Settling in our rooms and having a quick bite to eat in the cute kitchenette, we went back out to scout around. The water was calmer than the ocean. Wading in it, we were disappointed with the fact that it was still too cold for swimming, although the kids dared each other and quickly came out of the water, as their skin was turning blue. It was also getting toward evening and the air was cool. Again, we picked up some nice rock and shell specimens. Walking by the inlet docks, we watched as a fishing party boat came in and unloaded a great catch of fish.

Friday morning (the 19th), after a hearty breakfast at the motel, we headed north. Stopping at the airport in Norfolk, we spent some time watching the huge airliners come and go. Back in those days it didn't take much to amuse children, nor grown-ups! Norfolk was getting ready for its azalea festival, so as we drove through, we saw many beautiful lawns crowded with azalea blooms - dogwood trees were blooming also - and many other Spring flowers.

We headed away from the coast as we went on the Hampton Roads Bridge Tunnel to Hampton, and toward Washington, D.C. Stopping at Jamestown along the way, we toured through this historic town, and learned that after many other efforts along the Atlantic coast, the English succeeded in establishing its first lasting settlement in Jamestown. Driving up through another historical town, Williamsburg, we continued on and found a motel just before Washington.

Saturday morning we arrived at the Washington Monument. We decided to climb up all the 898 steps to the top - except Bill, Sr. His excuse being, "I want you to take a picture from up top as I stand by the car, and I'll wave so you know what car it is!" What a joke and good excuse! We did take the picture of the station wagon and Bill, who was the size of an ant. The capitol building was having a face-lift, so one more thing we couldn't go in. We spent a short time at the Smithsonian Institute and saw many interesting things. We didn't stay in Washington very long since there had been a racial outbreak just two weeks before. We saw many buildings and homes boarded up where windows had been broken.

On a northerly route, we skirted around Baltimore, Maryland, and came to Wilmington, Delaware. There was supposed to be a 'kiddie' park and zoo in the area. After scouting around for over an hour, we finally found it. The place was closed! It was being repaired and painted for the summer season! So, again, onward. Over the Delaware Memorial Bridge to the New Jersey Turnpike, then crossing over South Jersey to Waretown where Bill's sister had a Summer home. We had called ahead of time to ask if we could use the bungalow for the night.

Sunday morning, bright and early, Bill took the three boys fishing out on Barnegat Bay. All four 'boys' were happy with that idea. I got in touch with my sister, Mauvline, who lived ten miles away, and she told me where I could take the girls horseback riding in Lakewood. We all enjoyed our last morning and didn't want to head home. We did though, arriving quite tired from the six-hour drive late in the evening.

Monday morning five weary children boarded the school bus, reluctantly. I do know they had some wonderfully exciting stories to tell to their friends and teachers. Tommy couldn't wait to tell about all of the bridges he went over, and their sizes. The older boys had reports about the interesting tour of NASA on Wallops Island. As for the girls, their favorite things were the horses and the different shells found.

Bill and I made it a point each year after that trip to take a family vacation, usually for the two weeks around Easter. We also made sure we would go further south where it would be warmer, and we could all do some swimming in the ocean or bay, rather than just look at the beaches. Many times we rented a pop-up camper and stayed at State or National parks where excitement abounded, whether at Atlantic Ocean beaches, or in the mountains of West Virginia, Kentucky, the Carolinas, or Georgia. We used to laugh at my mother when she took my younger sisters on trips. When her money was half gone, she would head back home. Bill and I found ourselves doing the same thing. We would usually get as far south as Florida. In 1972 we were at Disney World when it first opened. None of the kids minded buying Florida tomatoes to put on bologna sandwiches at a picnic table in some park, and washing it down with Kool-Aid - as long as we could afford to buy the tickets for Disney World.

Of course, there was no place nicer to vacation during the summer than in our own back yard in the country on the western slopes of the Catskill Mountains!!

Chapter

ROMANCE IN THE CATSKILLS

B eing a widow for quite some time, my Mom was used to living her own life. She had retired to Florida for a few years, but missed family, and decided to come back north. I had a brother and three sisters living in New Jersey, but when Bill and I offered to have her come live with us in the Catskills, she really appreciated it. We let her set up a mobile home on our property a couple of hundred yards from our house. She became rather content living in the mountains.

Sometimes Mom and I would walk up in the back fields, picking berries or wild flowers along the way. Other times we'd go for a drive and explore back roads of the area and surrounding towns. And, of course, there were many trips to the big town of Oneonta to go shopping.

Mom got into the habit of walking out to the end of our long driveway to the mailbox. One day, in late summer, she came to the back door with the mail. We sat by the picnic table on the patio. Mom had a big grin on her face, and there seemed to be a twinkle in her green eyes.

"I just met Roy, the mailman," she said. "You never told me he was around my age!"

"I never thought of it, Mom," was my weak reply.

"And you never mentioned he was a widower!" she added.

"No, I guess I haven't." I said, sheepishly.

Several days later she came up on the patio, giggling like a young schoolgirl.

"Roy stopped at the mailbox and asked me to go out to dinner with him!" Mom revealed with a fluster.

"That's nice, Mom. Where are you going to go?"

"Oh, I didn't tell him if I would yet," she sounded cautious. "I don't want to go out on a real date....and I don't want him to get serious."

"Mom, go out with him, have some fun! Enjoy a dinner with someone your own age for a change." I encouraged her. "What harm is there? So, don't get serious!"

A few days later Roy came to pick Mom up. It was fun peeking out of our window and watching him escort her out to his car. Mom started to walk to the mailbox every day just in time to meet Roy. Sometimes with an umbrella if it was raining. They were going out for dinner more often and for drives through the lovely countryside.

"Mom, this doesn't look so casual anymore. You and Roy are doing some serious dating lately!" I joked with her one day.

Her face was all aglow as she said, "He took me to meet his family last night. Did you know he has five sons?"

Yes, I did know it. I knew Roy had lost his wife about ten years before Mom moved here. I also knew Roy and his wife had their five sons late in life, and a couple of them had dated my daughters off and on when they were still at home with us. Roy was a Bovina Center hometown resident since he was nine years old. His folks were farmers, but then, they gave up the farm as their family went on to other endeavors. Roy became a truck driver, and when retiring from that job, he became the rural route mailman. He traveled over 50 miles each day to the back road folks. Everyone knew Roy. Back in those days people would call him up and ask if he could please stop at the store and get them a loaf of bread, or a dozen eggs, or maybe butter, and deliver it with the mail. Roy was glad to help out people in that way. (Don't forget, this was the 'olden' days of the 60's and 70's.) As he delivered the mail, he'd find the money in the mailbox for the groceries.

A few more weeks went by when, one day, Mom came in to let us know that Roy asked her to marry him.

"I don't want to rush into this," she said. "I told him to wait until spring. This way we can get to know each other better."

Being October, I thought it a good idea. But a week later she came all excited saying, "Roy wants to get married sooner. I said 'yes', but to wait till January, after the Holidays."

"Are you sure about this Mom?" I asked.

Another week went by, and I saw her scurrying past our front window, sloshing through a late October snowfall, in her black galoshes (can you remember those things?). As she came up the back driveway and onto our patio I went to open the door for her.

"Why the rush, Mom? What's the matter?" I questioned.

"Roy can't see why we have to wait to get married. He wants us to enjoy the coming Holidays together! He thinks it would be great with our combined families. What do you think I should do, or say?" she asked.

"Mom, what do YOU think you should do? What do you WANT to do? How do YOU feel about the whole idea? Do you love him enough?" I asked question after question.

She finally caught her breath as we sat down with a cup of hot tea to discuss the situation.

"He's right!" she said. "We enjoy each other, we enjoy going to the same places together. We need companionship, and most of all, we do feel a love for each other. Besides, I'm going to be 73 next week and he's 70. Who knows how many more Holidays we'll be able to spend together?!"

The date of December 8, 1979, was chosen. Barely six weeks to get a wedding together. My brother and three sisters lived over 200 miles away back in New Jersey. As I called them, one by one, they responded with the same outburst! "What?".... "Mom getting married?".... "I don't believe it!!"

Flowers were ordered. Invitations were hand-made, addressed, and sent. The cake was ordered. Mom found a lovely light blue dress that set off her silvery-white hair. She honored me by asking to be her matron of honor. Roy chose one of his sons as best man. The Bovina Center church became ready for the big event. The ladies of the church very graciously offered to cater the reception-dinner in the church basement. All of the towns-people including those on the mail route wanted to help with the occasion. Roy had a big family just as excited and eager to help. After all, who ever thought back then about marriage when you are over 70 years old??

If only the weather would hold out. In the Catskills the weather was never too co-operative in December. The big day came with gray dreary clouds. Snow, with traces of sleet, kept swirling down. It wasn't a very nice day. But inside the church we didn't need the sunshine. There were many, many beaming faces. One hundred invitations had been sent out, one to a family, so with all the children, there were more than a hundred beaming faces. Over forty friends and relatives came the 200 miles of slick roads from New Jersey. Local friends and relatives mingled with the out-o'-staters to make it a truly joyous day!

After a week's honeymoon in Cooperstown and visiting Howe's Cave they came back to live in Roy's mobile home three miles down the road from us. My husband and I would 'check' on them a few times a week, or Mom would give me a call. Roy retired from delivering the mail a few years later. They both slowed up a bit, but enjoyed going to bingo games once in a while, or to a movie, or taking a drive to visit someone. Sometimes Martha (Mom) sent Roy to town for groceries or to get a haircut, knowing he'd find some old cronies to gab with....that way she could watch her favorite soap opera or quietly read a magazine.

Bill and I became sno-birds (migrating to Florida for the five months of Winter). We asked Roy and Mom if they would like to do the same, and, of course, they accepted our offer. They enjoyed the sno-bird life, appreciating the warm sunshine and the aroma of orange blossoms, knowing that the Catskills were inundated with snow and ice. Since Roy was a Catskill country boy, he had never seen the ocean. What a joy it was to watch him put his feet in the sand and then in the Atlantic Ocean waves. Another sight he couldn't get over was when we took a side trip and traveled over the Chesapeake-Bay-Bridge-Tunnel highway of 17 miles. He couldn't understand how a bridge could turn into a tunnel until we finally approached one of the tunnels. We stopped at the end of the one tunnel that had a pier and restaurant, which truly amazed him, as he watched ships sail over the spot where the tunnel was. But, by the end of April the four of us would get a longing for the mountains and were happy to get back 'home'.

Roy and Martha (Mom) Hadley enjoyed their married life together. But, the Christmas of 1993, Mom fell and broke a hip, and never fully recovered from it. By then, Roy had a problem with dementia, and he had chronic bone weakness. They both became wheel-chair bound. It was a heart-breaking responsibility of being given the power-of-attorney for both of them. Eventually I had to have them admitted to the near-by nursing facility. I must say, they enjoyed it together since they both shared the same room and received wonderful care. Many friends and relatives would visit them. By then, some of Roy's old friends were in the same facility and they would wheel around to visit each other.

One sad day in July of 1994 I had to give them the devastating news that my husband, Bill, had succumbed to a heart attack (at the age of 66)! They both were able to attend his memorial service at church in their wheelchairs....thanks to loved ones who helped them in and out.

Then in July of 1996 Roy was being fed his breakfast by an aide, who later told me that he just took a deep breath, laid his head back on his pillow, and decided it was time to meet the Lord. He was then buried in Bovina Center next to his first wife. Mom, rather ironically, died on their 16th anniversary, December 8, also in 1996. Her ashes were strewn over the burial place of my father back in New Jersey.

This story is written for those who think marriage is probably out of the question when finding themselves single again in their 70's. Romance can come at anytime, at any place. It did in the hills of the Catskills. Hm-m-m.... I'm now in my 70's!!!

Chapter 14

BIRD

When my children noticed that I had become an avid bird watcher, one Christmas they thought they would give me a gift that I truly would enjoy. A BIRD. How could I refuse it? It was something I really did not want in the house! It was a parakeet. It was in a cardboard box. I told my husband that since he was part of this 'wonderful' surprise, it was his job to go out and find a bird cage....and bird seed! I tried to be pleasant in front of the kids, but in my mind was the thought of the daily care for this creature. Feeding, watering, and, of course, cleaning out the cage! YUK!! The birds that I loved to watch outdoors took care of themselves. Even if I didn't put out seed, they could find it in the fields and woods.

BIRD, for lack of a better name, was not one of my favorite pets. We had a dog and some cats that I always had to chase away from the cage. Except for the attention he received from the hissing cats, and my occasional feeding and cleaning him, Bird started to take matters into his own hands. Perhaps I should say claws. There were toys hung in the cage that he started to apply his antics on. He became well pleased with himself when he drew my attention by his frantic bobbing and jigging, and noisy chattering and whistling.

He loved to pull on the silver bell that was hanging on the bottom of his four-sided mirrored toy, which is hooked to the top of his cage. As the bell swung crazily back and forth, his game was to swing opposite of the bell, dodging it with his head, bobbing from side to side. His whole body would bob while hopping from one foot to the other. He became a bundle of action from the top of his blue-green head to the end of his black-tipped tail. Most of his green plumage, which he preened daily, was tipped with black. Pulling on the bell with his little curved beak, he would sometimes get rambunctious and pull too hard then forgot to dodge it; and was hit on the head by the returning silver bell. Taking hold of the clapper, he would shake it as if the whole toy would snap and break off! He would seem quite angry with that bop on the head.

A circular green plastic swing also hung from the top of Bird's cage. It had a radius of about four inches with a small bar across the bottom that he would perch on, and on one side was also a small, tinkling bell. He learned that he could sit on the perch with one foot and jiggle this bell with the other foot. The incessant tinkling was sometimes unnerving!

With all of that, Bird had also learned a variety of noises. Many times he would hop to one of the wooden perches along the bottom of the cage and imitate the swinging mirrored toy. By this, I mean that he bobbed back and forth from one foot to the other to the rhythm of the sounds from his throat which were a tick-tick, tick-tick, tick-tick, sounding like the chain hooked at the top; similar to that of a wound-up clock. He really captivated attention by that amusing trick!

If he heard a bird on the television or outside the window, he would start twittering and chattering and whistling as loud as he possibly could. When grandchildren came to play with some of their noisy toys, Bird would click and clack with his throat and tongue to the sound of the toys. If someone was rattling dishes, he hopped back and forth from one rung to another, chattering and twittering. The vacuum cleaner drove him almost wild and he would beat his feathery wings while hopping and jumping and shrieking.

Bird had certainly learned how to draw my attention. His antics were truly amusing. He became very interesting to watch, especially during the winter when there weren't too many outdoor birds to watch. The cage cleaning was no more a chore. When bird realized I paid more attention to him, he was beside himself in wanting to do more tricks. My unwanted Christmas present had made himself most welcomed!

Chapter 15

THE BARN RAZING

It had to be done. An element of danger was there. Visible memories would be erased, but the old barn just had to come down. Empty for several years, heavy snows had left their toll. The roof was partially caved in. It was an eyesore. The farm, at one time, was a beautiful place with its stately barn. Now, acres and acres of the property have literally been chopped into pieces of ten, maybe twenty, acres and sold off. My husband and I were able to buy the farmhouse and barn with fifteen acres. Not farmers, we used the barn and acreage for personal use. This was now in the town of Bovina, N.Y.

What apprehension when the bulldozer arrived! The operator knew he had a job to do, and he went right to it. The first section to feel the crunch was a room alongside the runway to the haymow. As it slowly came down, I pictured three little pigs we first housed in there. The cement floor was broken into bits from their penchant of digging with their snouts. They had an outdoor area with board fencing that they loved to break through to tear up the lawn. Finally, those nuisances became tasty dinner items. The pigs had been replaced by some hens and a rooster. The rooster became very domineering, not only with certain hens, but also with whoever decided to collect the eggs. There came a day when we had chicken (rooster) stew!

The next section of the barn to go was the part where one of our sons raised heifers for several years for a neighboring farmer. With new fencing around the pasture and the hay cut from the fields, we looked like a working farm at the time. What fun was had when the bales of hay were stored up in the haymow! The kids would jump from one stack of bales to another. Forts were made. It was a good place to take sleeping bags to "camp out" for a night. Looking back, I now realize the danger, the falls that could have been from balancing on beams, or jumping over holes in the flooring. In later years, traces of candle wax were found! Did flashlight batteries burn out? But, when I was a kid, didn't I do the same thing when my Dad was a dairy farmer??

The dozer then knocked into the old garage that was attached. It must have been built back when cars were the width of what compact cars are today. We moved here with a wide, four-door, green, '72 Chevrolet. The first time I pulled into the garage I tore the molding off both the car door and the garage door. My husband wasn't too happy with the Christmassy look of barn red scratches on the green car!

The old milk house crumbled down next. One year we had a chance to buy an expectant sow pig. The milk house, with its very thick concrete floor and cement block walls, was just the place to keep her. She was huge, but very docile. The night her babies were born was one of excitement and wonder. Pig after pig was born. When the eighth one arrived, it wasn't breathing. As I cleaned its face, it turned blue. But, finally, after rubbing its stomach and back, it started to breath. The mother wasn't the least bit interested as to what I was doing with her baby since she was still in the throes of giving birth. I continued working with that little one, but it did eventually die. It was very sad since I had a five-year-old granddaughter experiencing birthing for the first time. She then became infatuated with the rest of the piglets that were born. That mother gave birth to 13 babies!!! Amazing! The next morning we went out to see this new family once again. We never thought of the big, heavy mother rolling around in her hay-bed. But that is what she did during the night, and we found four more dead piglets that had suffocated with the mother's weight. Such a sad sight to see. The eight babies gave us enough work, though, in the weeks to follow. The mother would become almost wild in her efforts to protect them when anyone came near. After the babies were weaned, we decided that the mother would be more useful as sausage and bacon in the freezer. In due time, the little ones were sold when they became sizeable.

The bulldozer came to the last section, where we had raised a couple of steers for our own consumption. The first calf was named Lucky Beefsteak. Lucky almost became a pet. As he put on the pounds, he also grew a set of horns. One by one, the boards on the backside of his pen came off, revealing a stone wall. Many times he broke out, only to be found grazing in the garden or on the lawn. One night we woke up to rather noisy "squeeeak, squeeeak,!" It was Lucky with his horns under the side of the car, rocking it as if ready to turn it over! Perhaps he was just sharpening his horns! It was the funniest thing to see Bill putting on a bathrobe over his shorts while running out in his slippers to get Lucky back in the barn! (At about 2 A.M.). One day our girls had friends over when they discovered Lucky loose. They scrambled every which way. Our twelve year old decided to take matters into her own hands. She went to the barn and came out with a pail full of feed. Nonchalantly, seven hundred pounds of beef, (including horns), trotted over to her. Meek as a lamb, he ate from the pail as she led him back to his pen and locked the gate. A few months later, Lucky wasn't so lucky as he provided us with many of his Beefsteaks.

More memories came into play as the barn razing continued. There was a time when the girls just had to have horses. There was a time when the girls realized that horses were hard work! Eventually, one horse turned into an old clunker of a car, and the other horse was replaced with an electric typewriter. Much more sensible and the girls were much happier with their "trade-ins". There was a horse-riding farm two miles away where they could go riding and didn't have to clean stalls or feed the horses.

The tall concrete block silo was last. It had metal rungs on the inside all the way to the top. Several grandchildren had once admitted to going up those rungs (they were ladder-like). Since it was located on the far side of the barn, I had never noticed that trick. The game was to see who could go the highest before getting "chicken"!! And I thought they were just playing out in the meadow. What a baby-sitter this grandmother was! The dozer operator dug a huge hole in the ground near the silo. Bit by bit the silo was crumbled and shoved into the hole, as was the splintered barn. The stone runway that once ushered hay wagons into the top mow was pushed onto the rubble. Mounds of soil were leveled over it, until the grading was completed.

What is left of the barn? Pictures. And memories. Wild flower seeds were spread and eventually wild poppies, bachelor buttons, black-eyed-susans, and several other meadow flowers were blooming there. This was another event to add to by-gone days of Catskill Mountain Memories. There were, at one time, six working farms on our three-mile country road. Now, there is only one. Three empty barns remain. Fourteen dwellings are on the road, some new, some original farmhouses. When old barns are razed, such as ours was, I hope it is just to relieve an eyesore, and to leave the countryside as a scenic and pleasant place. Many wonders still abound in those beautiful Catskills... you might see deer or wild turkeys or perhaps an elusive black bear!

Chapter 16

GRANDPOP MEETS THE GARDEN GNOME

This is just a little fictional story I wrote since my husband and I enjoyed gardening, and, Bill especially liked to tell the grandkids stories.

After we had planted the vegetable garden up behind our farmhouse, Grand-pop would sit in his lounge chair that was nestled against the huge trunk of the walnut tree and watch the garden grow. Although we couldn't understand how he watched things grow when his eyes were closed. As the days went by, the little green seedlings started to find their way out of the loamy ground. First, the radishes, then lettuce, carrots, green beans, beets, corn, and whatever else was planted. It was wonderful to see the little green shoots coming up. Grand-pop would hoe in between the rows to keep the ground soft and the weeds out.

We would also have to thin out the seedlings since we had the habit of planting too many seeds.

One year Grand-pop started to notice rabbit tracks in the garden, but nothing seemed to be eaten. He then noticed, a few days later, that some of the vegetable rows were thinned where we hadn't worked on them. What was going on?? The tough, outer leaves of cabbage and Swiss-chard had been removed. Grand-pop could see where nibbles had been taken here and there. Nothing was really destroyed. The corn was thinned just right so there was six inches between each seedling, as it should be. The same thing was happening with the green beans as those plants became larger. Who was sneaking into our garden without a trace, except for the rabbit prints??

One evening Grand-pop decided to stay motionless in his chair, with his eyes barely open. At dusk the rabbits appeared noiselessly. Then, Grand-pop noticed something red. It wasn't any higher than the rabbits. It looked like an upside-down ice-cream cone! He couldn't believe his eyes! A little man wearing the red cone appeared, no higher than six inches tall! He had on a blue jacket, green pants, and black boots. The little creature was pulling up the plants here and there and feeding them to the rabbits, as if he knew all about gardening. Grand-pop wanted to rub his eyes, thinking he was dreaming.... he remembered some of the stories he told his grand-kids about little people called gnomes. A man from Holland had created the stories, and in his books he painted the gnomes just like the one that Grand-pop was watching. Grand-pop's father had come to the

United States from Holland when he was a boy of 16, and he would tell the gnome stories. This was too much for Grand-pop to take in.

As he was about to get up and shake himself from the unbelievable sight, the little gnome stepped closer, not seeing Grand-pop, as he was busy with the rabbits. Grand-pop lunged at the little mirage and caught him by his coat-tails. The rabbits went skittering every which way as the gnome flailed his arms when Grand-pop wrapped both hands around him. It was quite a sight! I think if Grand-pop had a red coned hat and a bushy, white beard, he'd be looking at his twin, although the gnome was only six inches high (and his hat was almost the same height!) As the gnome was shouting to the rabbits, Grand-pop was surprised to hear him speaking English. Calming the tiny man, Grand-pop started to talk to him.

"Are you a real person? Are you some thing from my imagination? What are you? Who are you?" He had so many questions; he didn't know when to stop.

"Since you are holding me so tightly, and I can't escape, I guess I'll have to tell you," said the little man. "My name is Cornelius, but I'm called Cornel, since I am a garden gnome and I enjoy thinning out the gardens, especially the sweet corn patches."

"How in the world did you get here?" asked Grand-pop. "I thought gnomes were fairy tale figures for bed-time stories in the country of Holland. If I ease my grip on you will you stay and tell me your story?"

"And would you let me continue to help in your garden and feed my friends, the rabbits?"

Grand-pop agreed.

"It's been many years," Cornel started. "About 350 years ago my family would help in the gardens in the old country, that is, the country of Holland, when I was very young. One day I roamed away from my family when they weren't looking...I knew I shouldn't, that I would get a good lickin', but I did. I didn't intend to go far, I was just exploring. But, then I saw a cow in a cage, and as it is with all our kind, I wanted to help that poor animal. I wanted to free him from the cage. I tried to call my family, but they didn't hear me. Getting into the cage I climbed up to the lock, and, as I was trying to reach to open it, some men came along, as big as you!! I never saw humans before then, being protected by my mother. I hid in the hay that was in the cage for the cow. Then I felt the men moving the cage! Being so frightened I kept under the hay. After a while when everything stopped, I peeked out. We were floating on water!

"I had no idea of what to do! I wanted to cry for my folks! I wanted to jump out of the cage! But I had no idea where to go. I can tell you now that we were floating on a barge and heading to open water near the sea. Eventually, the cage was lifted up into a huge ship. For a young gnome as I was, it was rather exciting, but, yet, it almost scared me to death!! There were a few other animals in cages, also another cow or two, and quite a few humans. You would call them people. You would also call them Puritans. After many weeks on the treacherous sea, we landed. I have never seen another family like mine since then. Not one Gnome family. Being so very small, I found my way to a hole under the roots of a huge tree. I scared a family of rabbits, but convinced them that I could be very helpful to them. And I was. As the Puritans made their gardens I would pick choice green seedlings, just as I did in your garden, and feed the rabbits. I taught them which ones to pick for themselves. I also found traps that the humans set for the animals and would guide them around the deadly things. We had to be wary of the animals called foxes. And deer, being docile and friendly, would let me get thorns out of their hooves, and ticks out of their hides, especially around their eyes. There was also a different kind of group of humans I wasn't sure of. The Puritans called them Indians. Over the course of years and much fighting, the Indians became rather sparse."

"After many years of wandering, and looking for my family, and visiting with that first cow, I somehow arrived here and settled on this farm. I resigned myself to helping whatever animals needed me. And, I know you won't believe me as to my age. To tell the truth, gnomes do not start families until they are about 250 years old. And then they only have one set of twins. As you can see, I have missed out on that blessing!" The little gnome ended his story with a sad look on his face.

"That is quite a tale, my friend, Cornel, but, 350 years ago?? That seems impossible. And landing at where? Plymouth Rock? Or there about? And you drifted up here into the Catskill Mountains from there??? It's hard to believe!" said the elderly man. "But, if that's your story, so be it! It's a good one to tell the grandkids. But, as for Grandma, I'm not so sure!!" he chuckled.

So Cornel stayed on the farm and helped wherever he could. There came a day though, when Grand-pop told him he was going south on a camping vacation for the winter. Cornel had gotten so used to helping not only the animals, but Grand-pop, and having conversations with him, that he felt sad when he saw the elderly couple packing the camper and truck. Cornel, the garden gnome secretly hid in the bed of the truck, behind some luggage and the toolbox.

It was quite a long trip for the garden gnome. Much longer than coming up to the Catskills from the northeast. Finally, after a couple of days, Grand-pop parked the truck and set up the camper, with the help of Grand-mom, in a wonderful woodland park near the ocean. Cornel was hoping they weren't going on that ocean as he did many years ago. Grand-pop and Grand-mom were getting a fire started on the grill and bringing out lounge chairs and fishing poles, so it seemed to Cornel that they were settling in at this camp-ground. It was then that he decided to sneak out of his hiding place and, once again, go exploring.

After many months of enjoying the warm southern winter, it was time for Grand-pop and Grand-mom to pack up and go back north. They had no idea that Cornel had come south, so never looked for him. Again, it was time to plant the gardens. By then Grand-mom knew about Cornel, so as the couple planted the seeds in the rows they had made, they planted many extra seeds, as they kept looking for signs of the little gnome.

Grand-mom was beginning to doubt the story, "Seems I never see a red-coned hat when I am up here helping you, Pop," she said one day.

"I knew it was something you wouldn't believe, that's why I never told you about him till that one day when we were camping. Now, I'm sorry I told. It's hard even for me to believe now!" Grand-pop answered.

Weeks later, as the seedlings were starting to show, Grand-pop was getting nervous, thinking the rabbits and other foragers would be coming to mess up the garden. But, then, as he was sitting in his chair by the old walnut tree, he saw a flock of Canada geese, that seemed late in their flight north. The flock landed to rest at the pond across the road. The elderly man picked up his binoculars that he always had at hand, and watched as one goose in particular wing his way to the far side of the garden. On the goose's back was a red conical shape, and in back of it was a green cone!! As the goose landed there was Cornel sliding off it's back along with a female gnome who was wearing the green cone-shaped hat! Again, Grand-pop couldn't believe his eyes!!

After the Canada goose flew back to the flock by the pond, Grand-pop lumbered over to where the little couple was standing, frightening the little plump female gnome. Cornel held onto her hand and explained that the man was a friend. She still seemed unsure of the big figure as he towered over the two of them.

Cornel put his arm around her as he said, "This is the Grand-pop that I told you about."

"Cornel, I didn't think I'd ever see you again after we left you here to get through the winter," Grand-pop exclaimed.

"I must confess to you that I took that trip with you to the South. I hid in the back of the truck on your terribly long journey, but stayed with you and the Mrs. all the way," Cornel said. "Then, when you were settling into the camp-site, I once again took to exploring."

Grand-pop got down on his knees and inquired of Cornel, "and just who do you have here, my friend?"

Cornel's cheeks became a bit more rosy as he explained, "This is Violet. She is from a woodland family of gnomes. As I explored around the campsite, I went deeper into the woodlands, and then deeper and deeper. I found some deer and rabbits, and even raccoons, to attend to that needed some help. They told me of other gnomes like me that had helped them! It was wonderful to hear that other families were around. One of the deer had me ride on his back and went deeper yet, into the woods. We found quite a few gnome families there. They told me about coming across the ocean on sailing vessels, secretly, and landed on the shores of what is now known to be the oldest city of this country, St. Augustine."

"We visited that city this past winter, Cornel. It's amazing you were nearby and I never knew it." Then

Grand-pop informed him, "I told Grand-mom about you, but since you hadn't shown up in the garden this year, she is doubting my story. But, now, what have you to say for yourself about this little lady whose hand you are holding so tightly!!"

"Gramps," Cornel said with a tone of familiarity, "I thought you would never ask! Although from a Woodland family, Violet and I became rather friendly, so much so, that when I asked her to be my wife, she said 'yes' right away. The big problem was, of course, her family. They began to notice that we were very happy together. We had a wonderful wedding, and I suggested that we go on a honeymoon with the geese we were friendly with when they fly north. Violet's family wasn't too pleased with that idea! So, we promised them to come back with the Canada geese in the winter. Now every year when the geese arrive at the pond for a rest during their long flight they will either be picking us up or dropping us off. By the way, Grand-pop, did I ever tell you that gnomes only have one set of twins, a boy and a girl, during their married life-time? So, when we go on our trips the geese won't mind the 2 extra little ones."

Eventually, Grand-mom came out to see what was keeping Grand-pop so long in the garden and almost fainted when she saw what she thought she saw.

"Now there are two?! Pop! I can't believe what I see!!"

"It's O.K. Gram, believe it. This is Cornel and his bride, Violet. Come and say 'Hello' won't you?

They'll be staying till winter, so get used to them." Grand-pop warned.

Violet came from behind Cornel as Grand-mom took her hand and started talking to her. "So, you are Violet. What a lovely name as are those lovely woodland flowers."

Everyone became friendly all at once and started talking about gardens, and the seedlings, and the care of the rabbits, and perhaps, starting a Garden-Woodland gnome family in the near future. Of course, Grand-mom and Grand-pop could only tell the grandkids that the stories of gnomes are just fairy... oops... gnome tales, and not real. They will, undoubtedly, tell the kids to be on the lookout for an upside down red cone, or maybe a green one.

Chapter 17

THE OCKLAWAHA RIVER

No, there is no such river in the Catskills. But when my husband, Bill, and I retired we became 'sno-birds'. That's the way I spell that word, sno-birds. We decided to give up our farmhouse and bought two mobile homes. One for the six month winter season to spend in Florida, (I don't think we ever had a Spring or Fall in the Catskills.) The other six months we lived in the other mobile home nestled in the woods on the side of a mountain overlooking the second farmhouse we had lived in. We built a large two-tiered deck on the front of the home so as to look down the valley. This place had five acres to it so I could still view the wildlife and do some gardening. When I think of it, it was the best of times as we could enjoy our two different 'worlds'. We now joined the migrating monarch butterflies, the Canada geese, the robins, the hummingbirds, and, yes, the other human sno-birds.... But this story is about the Ocklawaha River in Florida.

We wintered in Summerfield, a small town near Lake Weir. We had a small boat with an outboard motor, and not knowing the area too well, we just kept going to the lake to do our boating and fishing. After several weeks and getting tired of the lake, we took a drive to do some sightseeing. Only ten miles from our winter home, we 'found' the Ocklawaha River. Coming to a small restaurant with a few cabins and campers in the back, we noticed this complex was on the edge of a canal leading to the river. There was a boat launch pad at the canal, so we asked about permission to put our boat in. The owner said he charges a dollar for each time!! Couldn't beat that!

The Ocklawaha River is one of the few rivers that flow in a northerly direction. Starting at Lake Griffin in Leesburg, the river flows up to Silver Springs, and then northeast to the St. John's River. We first explored the river northward. It was a very beautiful and pristine stretch of water. Lily pads and reeds jutted from the banks. Pockets of cypress knees and cypress trees could be seen in the brackish waters of riverside lagoons. After a few miles we came to a small park with a fishing dock, some picnic tables, a boat ramp, and, of all things, a lock! Deciding to experience passing through a lock we followed the directions of a sign near an abutment.... "Pull the Rope". We did, and a bell rang. We could hear water rushing in beyond the lock gates. Once filled up to the level of water we were floating in, the huge steel gates opened. Revving up the engine, Bill maneuvered the boat into the lock. Being the only ones to go in, we felt quite alone as the steel gates clanged together. Sitting there a few moments we suddenly heard water sloshing out. Slowly receding one foot, two feet, three, we noticed the walls of the lock had numbers of feet painted on them. We were intrigued as to how the lock worked. We were lowered over 30 feet in this now cavernous, echoing, cement- walled water trap. Heading out of the lock when the opposite gates finally opened, we started down river once again. Along the banks on the lower end were many fishermen, and women. Some seemed to be having great luck. Going further, there was nothing but wilderness. Wild flowers were blooming here and there, Spanish moss draped from the trees. Scrub palms and live oak trees abounded everywhere. Were we lost somewhere in Africa, or going along the Amazon?? It was just beautiful!!

Then we couldn't believe our eyes! What seemed like a log up ahead decided to sink just below the water surface and swim away! An alligator?? Yes! A little further we saw a smaller one sunning on the bank. How exciting! Noticing that we were getting close to Silver Springs, there were quite a few more boats. The water was getting much clearer, and we could see fish swimming. There were signs posted along the way that we couldn't go into the Silver Springs Attraction Park, but we met up with some of their sightseeing boats. Someone was pointing up into the trees near us. Looking up, we saw about a dozen monkeys in the wild! Unbelievable! Some boaters were throwing cookies and bread to them. We learned at a later time that these monkeys were families of those that had escaped from the springs zoo section a few years back. At this point we decided to turn around and head back home.

The next trip we took was in a southerly direction - upstream. Going out the canal from the boat ramp there were many water lilies blooming. We saw white egrets and a great blue heron. Getting out onto the Ocklawaha River once again, there were a few boats drifting along with people fishing from them. The sun sparkled where the fish were jumping. The banks held colorful blooming flora. The river became wider and more enticing. We noticed a pair of eagles flying by. Osprey were nesting on poles especially made for them. Some were overhead scanning the river for fish. There were more herons, and egrets; also gallinules, anhinga, all sorts of waterfowl. But it was the number of alligators that amazed us, just floating on the water, some swimming. Boaters maneuvered around them with all due respect, but the 'gators showed no fear. Some were lying in the middle of the river, watching. Little inlets flowed into the river from small streams along the way. Up those small streams we couldn't tell if we were seeing fallen logs or more alligators sunning themselves. As the river kept widening, small islands appeared. All had alligators. Coming to the mouth of the river where it formed at Lake Griffin, we turned back and enjoyed the beauty of the approximate ten miles doubly. We had to admit that first trip to the lake was a bit scary!!

After that, we became quite familiar with the river waters, joining other fishermen, trying our luck among those alligators. But Bill and I received the most enjoyment taking our visiting northern friends and relatives for a ride on the Ocklawaha. The grand-kids were especially excited. They all had to agree it was more exciting seeing everything in the wild rather than at a theme park. We would try to get as close as possible for picture taking. We all enjoyed traveling up and down this stretch of river called the Ocklawaha with its spectacular glimpses of the semi-tropical flora and fauna.

Oh, yes! I must tell about the little restaurant where we launched the boat. It did have a bar where fishermen could tell their stories about the big one that got away. But it also had a screened in porch facing the canal where we would find a table to sit at, to watch the boats coming in and going out. This place had the best hamburgers. The man who did the cooking would always take the fresh meat and form the large burgers by hand. He grilled them just right and put them on large rolls with whatever else you wanted on them. But, the one thing I noticed, was that he was the same man who would go out back of the building to put bait - whether minnows, worms, grass shrimp - into containers that we bought for fishing. The big question we always asked ourselves, espe-cially when we had our friends there....did this man ever wash his hands after handling all the bait before he made the hamburgers??? But we had to admit; we never got sick from those wonderful hamburgers!!

Chapter 18

CHANGE IN CATSKILL COUNTRY

Change was mentioned in one of the previous chapters of this book; but looking back in my files, I have found this story I had written back in 1983. Perhaps you will enjoy reading it as I had clarified the changes with more depth. More than 20 years have passed since I wrote this, so, I am sure more change has happened in the Catskills as it has in our lives.

Change. Are you afraid of change? Most people are. The change of home, job, environment, is a big step. Once made, you wonder why you didn't make it sooner.

When we decided to change our lifestyle, my husband and I and our five children lived in a busy, growing town in New Jersey. We pulled up our roots and planted them in a very rural section of Catskill country. We found an old farmhouse that was empty and just waiting for us to move in.

We were used to having neighbors within 100 feet on either side of our home. In the Catskills the nearest house was a mile away. In New Jersey our kids would go out the back door and our yard became filled with a half dozen more kids. In the Catskills they learned to play and become friends with each other, not seeing other children for days except at school. In New Jersey the children had 30 to 40 class-mates in each class. In the Catskills they were lucky to have 20, and that was due to double classes. In New Jersey we walked a half-mile to a store for any item we needed. In the Catskills the nearest country store was three miles away, larger stores about 15 miles away. Afraid of change? Maybe so....but we became used to it, and learned to love it.

Very fortunately, we came to Catskill Country (settling just outside of East Meredith which you probably can't find on the map) the same year the South Kortright Center for Boys opened; 1963. This was a state school for delinquent boys. My husband, Bill, applied for a job and was accepted to start right in to work there. It took him 45 minutes to drive the 22 miles to the school. Can you imagine how long it would take in New Jersey with the 'bumper to bumper' rush hour traffic? In New Jersey Bill was a cop, arresting juvenile delinquents and sometimes putting them behind bars. In South Kortright he helped to rehabilitate them so they could be released to the outside community. It was a more rewarding change.

Don't think I am knocking New Jersey. I'm not. We enjoyed its mountains, lakes, pinelands, and especially the ocean beaches with its' bays and deep-sea fishing. Bill still can't take to fresh water fishing. Our problem (or was it just mine?) was that we couldn't, (or wouldn't), put up with the busy-ness of the area where we lived. We looked to move to a rural spot in New Jersey, but then we heard of the place in the Catskill Mountains. All it took was one trip to the area and we knew it was for us. I have noticed of late, many cars with N.J. license plates here in the Catskills. Perhaps the people are just vacationing, or perhaps they own some of the little retreats that are now dotting the hillsides. Perhaps they are tired of the busy-ness, of the daily bumper-to-bumper traffic, and of tripping over neighbors. Perhaps they are looking for a change.

Putting the shoe on the other foot, I know that it's been hard for the 'home-town' folks of the mountains to get used to the influx of 'out-of-towners', and especially 'out-of-staters'. When we first came to Catskill country we were welcomed by several friendly neighbors, but others were quite distant, and I don't mean in miles. It took a while to become accepted. After 10 years, in 1973, we moved to a farmhouse three miles from the boys school and five miles outside of Bovina Center in the opposite direction. (Bovina being another town hardly found on the map.) Again, we had to get used to hometown folks reluctance. This town had every right to be reluctant since the place we moved into, with its' 15 acres, was once part of a large and beautiful 600 acre farm that was literally chopped into many little pieces of 10 or 15 acre parcels. This created much upheaval not only for those who bought the properties, but the road department, the tax assessors, the building codes, and other departments. The one good thing that came out of all this was a town planning board, which has been very helpful with the changes being now made in the town of Bovina.

After 12 years in Bovina, I find myself reluctantly accepting newcomers, when I should be happy for them. They are setting out to look for a change of life-style as we did. I'm beginning to feel like the hometown natives in reluctantly accepting the changes throughout the countryside. I wonder how many 'natives' realize that many years ago I went through what they are now going through?! I was born and raised on a farm in New Jersey. There is no sign of that farm now. It is inundated with apartment buildings, condominiums, and streets. Now, that is some change!! Perhaps you can understand why I appreciate living here. Catskill Country is beautiful, serene, peaceful.

In the 23 years we have been in this area, we have seen many changes. There has been centralization of several school systems, expansions at colleges, new shopping centers, new public buildings, new factories, highway expansions, and many, many new homes. This has not, as yet, taken place in the immediate areas of Meredith or Bovina, but within a 30, 40 & 50 mile radius. Change is inevitable. Even though we do not like some changes, we must be ready to accept them. With many small family farms pushed out of business, these families must make the change to learn new jobs. Many new jobs are in construction. This is due largely to 'city-folk' looking for the same serene, peaceful beauty that we have found.

Our children have all left our nest now, and are married. They have grown to love the area as much as we do. There is something about the mountains that is fascinating and alluring. Whenever we go away on a trip (even to the sunny south), as much as we enjoy it, we are always glad to be back home in the Catskills.

We are now going through another change. Bill has retired from the Boys Center this year. Our friends back in New Jersey are wondering if we will be moving back to their 'civilized' world. The fast lane is not for us. We have adjusted to all of our changes very well. We have come to love the area. There are many things ahead of us that we want to attempt to do that we haven't had a chance to do as yet. We may not succeed in everything, but we like challenge, and we have learned to cope with whatever change comes along....as long as we can face it here in the Catskill Mountains!

As mentioned in the first paragraph, more than 20 years have passed since I wrote this article on 'Change' In a different chapter, or two, I wrote that Bill passed away from a heart attack in 1994, and I now live in Ocala, Florida....a big change for me.

Chapter 19

A SMALL TOWN ANNIVERSARY FESTIVAL

Back in the mid-seventies, when we moved to our second farmstead in the Catskills, it was outside a small village called Bovina Center. The village was nestled at the bottom of what was called Bovina Mountain. Our home was three miles up the mountain of approximately 2000 feet. We were very much out in the country. We enjoyed the scenery with its hills, streams, and dairy farms scattered here and there. The main two roads crossed each other through the valley and followed beautiful sparkling streams. Bovina Center was in and around the fork of the roads. County Rte. 6, named Main Street, of course, wound through the village.

Years ago Bovina Center must have been a little bustling village, with several stores, churches, and schools. Some schools in the outlying areas consisted of just one room. By the time we moved to the Center

there was only one church left, and a small post office
in a room set off by itself housed in the post-master's
own home. Two stores were operating then; a feed
and parts and supplies store for the farmers, which
eventually closed...and the general store that sold
groceries, clothing, shoes, ice cream, penny candy,
and anything else you might think you would need.
The store was owned by an elderly couple, who had
a daughter, who helped. The daughter had gone on
to college, but quit and gave up her dreams when
she realized her parents needed help. Never married,
she kept the store open after her parents died until
she also died at the age of eighty-something. The
store has since been donated to the Bovina Historical
Society. The members faithfully polished up the old
pot-bellied stove, the old cash register, the butcher-
block counter, and the penny candy cabinet with its
curved window covering. The Historical Society also
keeps the first firehouse in shape and a small building
that houses many antique artifacts from the towns
people, including an old fire wagon. It also sees to
the up-keep of a one-room schoolhouse.

A larger building in the village that was an elemen-
tary school is now the town library since the schools
have been consolidated in the nearby county seat of
Delhi. There is a great selection of books, and there
is a display case where people can put their artwork.
I once had my collection of gnomes displayed there.
A car repair shop is still in the village with a couple
of old fashioned gas pumps in front. Oh, yes, the
general store had gas pumps also, but gas became
too expensive for that family to continue with that

commodity. An old feed mill has been turned into an auction house that is quite popular for miles around. Many people have gone away with a treasure bought for a dollar or two that I know was worth twenty or thirty times that much.

Being about a four-hour drive from New York City many 'city folk' have been buying up the abandoned farms and other parcels of land; building vacation homes on them. There are many pristine ponds and streams in and around the mountains, which make for idyllic havens for retreats. The vacation homes were, at first, for Summer get-aways, but with ski centers nearby, and the craze for snow mobiles, Bovina is also busy with vacationers through the winter. Trout season is great in the spring, as is hunting season in the fall. Many of the older city folk have retired in Bovina or nearby towns in the Catskills.

The people of Bovina Center were, at first, dubious of strangers. They were close knit, many related to each other from generations past. But once they realized that people came to enjoy the peaceful surroundings, they become as friendly as you are. The Center has its own volunteer fire department and emergency squad. It has a well-equipped road department. I remember when sometimes we'd have a two or three feet snowfall overnight, the snow plows were out early in the morning since the schools were rarely closed except for extremely bad weather. I also remember that since we lived out on the farm and had to drive our kids a mile to where the school bus came to pick them up, we'd hear the town snow plow making a couple of swipes in and out of our long driveway (even though they weren't supposed to!).

The fire department had an annual chicken bar-b-que that people would come to from miles around, knowing the great reputation the men had for their special sauce. They also boiled hundreds of ears of sweet corn picked fresh from one of the farmer's own field. The wives would get together to make salads from their homegrown veggies. They'd also make hundreds of cupcakes. Everyone looked forward to this special event.

I remember one cool day when we had a chimney fire. Living three miles out of the village those volunteers were out to our place in minutes. They'd drop anything they were doing....milking cows, plowing, haying, mowing. Fortunately, we had no real damage to our home. We praised the Lord for those firemen!

Family circumstances had us move to Virginia after our twenty-year stay in Bovina, but we would always go back for a yearly visit. In 1995 Bovina Center had a special occasion. Its 175th Anniversary. I attended the event with old friends from the area. What a wonderful time. At first, there was the town parade. The Delaware County Sheriff's Department started the parade, proudly riding their horses. The Bovina Fire Department volunteers, all decked out in uniforms were next to march down Main Street followed by the Emergency Squad. The Bovina library association had a cute float with children posing reading books. The books were made as large as the kids, and some had large 'book-worms' going through them. A novel idea (if you get my pun). The church, on a wagon, was decorated beautifully and had family members reading Bibles. Most of the floats were on hay wagons pulled by farmers' tractors. Some wagons were just full of kids having a good time. Some wagons had kids with their pet animals that had ribbons on them, perhaps won at a fair, including calves, goats, chickens, pigs. Most of the wagons had the farm family name on them. Then there was a farmer and helper walking his herd of eight long-horned cattle on the road.

The parade dispersed at the end of a side road in a huge field near a hill. The sight itself was beautiful with the green trees and newly mown, lush green, hay field. Tents had been set up for people to eat that wonderful chicken bar-b-que and all the trimmings. There were many exhibits in the field: the old fire department trucks, many old and classic cars, farm equipment, especially tractors of all sizes and ages, and construction equipment owned by one of the families that ran its business outside of town. The Historical Society had its buildings open for all to view the displays of artifacts, such as old-fashioned clothing, baby carriages, old kitchen tools and appliances. Many families had stitched quilt squares depicting scenes of Bovina Center, and sewed them together to form a town quilt which was hung in the museum for display. There were other groups from neighboring towns that came to march in the parade....fire departments, emergency squads, old-time trucks and cars.

One group, the Hobart bag-pipers, marched into the field and formed a circle and performed on their instruments. They were dressed in their plaid kilts and green tams and did a marvelous job. After eating, the bag-pipers once again formed a circle to entertain us and a cloud opened up and drenched everyone. People came from all corners with umbrellas to hold over the pipers, and surprisingly, they continued their musical renditions proudly, even though getting a wee bit wet. A men's quartet from another town got together under the bigger tent and entertained everyone with their music, also. They were just a small town group that sang in local venues, but they knew how to harmonize very well. It was quite a memorable time.

Now living in Florida, I still drive back up there to the Catskill Mountains during the summer to visit the beautifully green, lush countryside, where the weather is deliciously cool. Bovina....a town for vacationers, dairy cows, and wonderful friendly people.

Chapter 20

MR. LOVE

I've kept this story for next to last, since it is rather sad. Yet, it is another way of life I had to learn while living in the Catskills.

We both seemed to know that this would be our last walk through the field together. The air was silent. Just the plodding of our feet through the brown grasses could be heard. It was late autumn here in the Catskills. The geese had already flown their southern routes. The robins and other songbirds were long gone. Every once in a while I could hear his labored breathing. It was late autumn in his life, too. I began to reminisce about the many walks we had taken together through these fields. Crossing the stream or sitting on top of a knoll, we would take in the beautiful scenery as we gazed down the valley road. Some evenings a full moon would be rising over the ridge before we walked back up the driveway to the farmhouse, and I enjoyed following our moonlit shadows as we entered the back door.

Sometimes I would bring a camera with me to take pictures of birds or colorful flowers, or autumn or spring budding leaves on the trees. He would wait patiently by my side. There was the time the two of us were sitting perfectly still near the stone wall as a young deer kept prancing nearby. It would curiously glance at my white cat strolling on top of the stone wall, and then nervously at my friend and me. As I quietly called the cat to come over to me, the deer was trotting behind it; and I was able to snap a picture of the deer before it ran off. My friend hardly flinched.

The name of my friend was Mr. Love. He was a big, lovable dog; part collie, part shepherd, (and possibly a few other things). He originally belonged to one of our daughters, who was the one who named him. When she married and then moved into town, she tearfully asked if he could stay on the farm where we lived, feeling he belonged here where he was used to roaming freely.

Taking this last walk with him, I thought of how many times I hunted in this field. Perhaps I aimed at that same deer after he grew up. I had fired at several woodchucks along this same trail. This time, I think Mr. Love knew why I was carrying the gun. It wasn't to hunt. Although how could he sense anything? He was so sickly this time. For the past few months he had large, ulcerated sores under his tail that I had kept medicating. He couldn't eat very well any more, and for the past few weeks he had become so dizzy he could hardly stand. His eyeballs seemed to spin. Even as we continued walking, he would reel over into a big heap after ten or fifteen steps. It took us well over a half hour to get to his favorite place at the edge of the field, which usually took ten or fifteen minutes. It was a clump of brush where he would romp and agitate woodchucks or rabbits, or just lie there in the heat of summer. He knew. He knew what was going to happen as soon as he lay there this time.

How many times have I killed chickens for our winter supply in the freezer? How many times have I helped our sow pigs with their birthing, only to help with the butchering of the young ones when they became of age? Can you imagine what cute little pets young pigs can become? We've had several cows killed and butchered that I've had no problems with….and many deer. How many times did we have to get rid of the 'critters' that were eating more than their share of our gardens? Then there were the cats! Where did they all come from? Especially the stray, expectant female cats. Were they really stray cats or were they dropped off by their owners who didn't want them when found pregnant?! After all, what better place to drop off cats up here in the country than at a farm?! A farm could always use another cat (or dog), couldn't it? That thought always made me angry!

Mr. Love had been with us for such a long time, seventeen years! I was feeling a bit queasy as I looked at him, but this is how it is in the country. This is how it is when family animal friends must go. This is the most humane way for the animal. He is in his own territory. Some of you may think it is hard-hearted. Maybe so. At least I know he is resting in one of his favorite places.

Looking into his eyes, he was no longer Mr. Love. They were eyes of a sick and dying animal....eyes that seemed to plead, "Hurry, I can't take this agony any more. Release me from this unending suffering!" With eyes pleading like that, I had to comply.

Mr. Love is not suffering anymore. Mr. Love is truly roaming free.

Chapter 21

WHATEVER HAPPENED TO THE "KIDS"??

(I am sure many of our mountain friends and
neighbors are asking that question.)

The move to the Catskill Mountains sounds as if
we were on vacation most of the time. Swimming
and fishing in the pond - skating and sledding and
tobogganing. Our friends and relatives would visit
and we would show them a great time. There were
baseball and football games, and volleyball, out in
the fields. But, vacationland to us? I don't think so!
Bill, my husband, had to go off to work. I had my
work cut out for me, and the five children had to
attend school. I think the biggest thing, though, was
that I thought we could leave the problems of urban
life behind us in New Jersey.

Even though we had a picket fence around our
back yard in New Jersey where our children had a

swing set, a sand box, and small swimming pool; as soon as they'd go out to play, we'd have three or four more children come into the yard. I didn't mind since it kept my kids busy, but I often wondered if they really had permission to come, or didn't their parents care where they were?! Once in a great while an argument would break out, then this 'meanie mommy' would have to send all the neighborhood kids home.

Living on a corner lot, we had a gate in the back fence facing the street. Being friendly with our neighbor, we had another gate put in between our two yards so the kids could go back and forth. But, then, when kids from across the street would come through our back gate, race across our patio to go to the next yard, they would not close the gates, which led to dogs coming in and out, and my little ones going out in the street. I think the biggest thing that bothered me, though, was when a neighbor from across the street had watched her boy run and trip up on our rather high cement step on the patio as he raced over to the next yard. She came over, knocked on my back door, and blatantly said, in all seriousness, "Kate, you realize if my child falls on that sharp step, I can sue you!!" That did it! Here I, more or less, was baby-sitting the neighborhood kids and had that slap in the face! My husband agreed with me to nail the gate closed on the neighbor's side, and then have a special lock on the one out to the street. I felt horrible about it, but that was how things were getting to be.

As the older boys were growing up, we gave them more freedom to go off with their friends either to the nearby park, a half-mile away, or to the store, about a mile away. We would hear stories about the boys grouping up with others, and then chase ducks or turtles in the park, or going along the nearby railroad track trying to knock signal lights in the overhangs with rocks. Sometimes they would dare each other to steal candy bars or other things at the store. With their father working as a policeman at that time, we'd be the first parents to hear the accusations. Once in a while we would get together with our neighbors in the evenings for coffee and cake and, perhaps, play cards, and chuckle over some of our kids pranks. But, then we women would usually get to fretting over the more serious problems. There was a time when one of the older neighborhood boys was running along the railroad. (Thank God our boys were not with him at that time!) He was so close to an on-coming freight train that the corner of the railing around the front of the engine clipped his head, tearing into it, and killing him. It was a horrible tragedy for our kids and for our neighborhood friends who lived just two doors away.

So, when Bill and I decided to make the move to the Catskill Mountains, it was a relief in my mind that we'd have some new adventures. Of course, I knew there would be other children there also. Did I think they would be better than those we were leaving? No. No better, and no worse, than what our own children were. But I did think it would take a while for ours to find problems. And it did!

The biggest problem for our children was when Bill and I changed our religion to a new and better life style of Christianity. Something the kids couldn't understand at first; Sunday School and church being top priority. Bible lessons and memory verses had to be done. "Mom, we have enough homework from school!" Then there were always two summer weeks of Vacation Bible School. Whatever children were visiting us would always come along, also.

I can't remember too much about Bill, Jr., who was basically, a good boy up in the Catskills. I always heard good reports of him when working for the neighbor farmers. For extra spend money he would raise young heifers for the farmers in our barns. His one problem when he first started school (in the village of Treadwell) was that he was behind in his grades. With the influx of children from other countries back in New Jersey, the teachers had a hard time teaching them English, so the local kids seemed to get pushed aside. The teachers in Treadwell were very dedicated in that they wanted to see their students get ahead. Young Bill, who was in the sixth grade when we moved there, received much help. The principal, himself, would spend his lunch hour helping Bill with some studies. Bill, Sr., and I were just amazed with this type of man. Bill, Jr., then went on to eventually graduate high school, and he and a friend enlisted into the Coast Guard. He served several years, came out, and took some courses in the local college where he met his wife. Did he ever get into any trouble? Sad to say, they both dabbled with pot for a while. Now, they are the only ones still living in the Catskills, along with their two married daughters nearby. Bill works at the wastewater treatment plant in Walton, but the love for hunting and fishing in the mountains is what is keeping him up there.

And then there was Ed!! Somehow, he was tagged Mama's boy. Why? I'm not sure to this day. Perhaps because young Bill was Grand-pop and Grand-mom Troost's boy. But Ed was the opposite of Bill. Always the little instigator, the antagonist; but with his big, blue eyes, he could win anyone over. Still does!! He was daring and stubborn. One time, when his brother, Bill, was trying to fix his bicycle, he had it upside down and oiling the chain. Bill would turn the pedals and Ed would put his finger on the chain. Bill said, "Stop!" Ed chuckled and put his finger on it again. Bill said, "Stop!" again. I don't know how it happened, but, one of Ed's fingers became caught in the chain, and the tip of it was mashed off almost to the first knuckle. I think he was only three or four at the time, but he had quite a set of lungs as he laid on the doctor's table, who was cleaning and stitching the finger! This was still in New Jersey. Bill has a small scar on his head where Ed retaliated with a shovel a few weeks later.

After our move to the Catskills, Ed seemed to really enjoy the new environment. In school he did quite well in all of his grades, especially in mathematics. He would lay on the floor in front of the television doing his homework. His father couldn't understand how he could watch the programs, yet, within a short time he'd hand his homework over, and it was completed. One day Ed showed a stubborn streak to his father while standing in front of the television. His Dad asked him, "Please, move away."

Ed then just rested his arm on the T.V. and kept his head half way in front watching the program. His Dad said, "Please, move away!" He did, but kept his hand on top of the T.V. By then, his father was turning red as he said, "Please, take your hand off!" Ed did, but kept his pinky finger on it. By then his father got up and swatted him on the behind!! If Bill, Sr., wasn't so serious about it, the whole episode was rather comical. But, that was Ed!

Ed was good, he was fun, he played the trumpet in the school band, and he liked playing baseball during high school. He's the one who raised pigs to help himself financially, and did well working on nearby dairy farms. Did Ed get into trouble while in the Catskills? I think trouble found Ed. While hiking with friends they came across some heavy road machinery. I never knew the full story, but some of those machines were moved, and one of the other fellows was blamed for it. There were hunting cabins that were broken into. By whom??? Then there was the time when Ed became of driving age and went to New Jersey to help an uncle who wanted to take his family on vacation. The uncle had a milk delivery business, delivering cartons of milk to the doors of his customers. (A thing of the past now.) Ed was to stay a week. He had a friend to help him. Not a good thing. Four or five days later the call came that he was in the hospital. He had an accident with the milk truck early in the morning. It seemed since he became old enough to drive, he thought he was old enough to pick up girls in the evening...therefore, fell asleep at the wheel of the truck. His father had to make a mad dash to N.J. while I had to stay home with the rest of the children. Bill tried to make up for the loss on the route. But Ed's uncle was never too happy with him after that since his business was ruined financially.

Ed graduated from high school with honors. A couple of years later he married a local girl whose dad was a retired Navy captain and a professor at the local college. His father-in-law convinced him that retirement from the military was a great thing financially, so Ed enlisted into the Air Force. After eight years it wasn't what Ed wanted, so he left the service, but had become well adapted to computers and worked for Texas Instruments in Dallas, Texas. He is now living outside of Dallas with his second wife, and is in partnership with a rather lucrative demolition company in the heart of Dallas.

As for Nancy, our third child - we were so happy to have a sweet baby girl after having two rough and ready boys. Bill was almost seven, and Ed was four and a half when Nancy was born. I just enjoyed dressing her in little girl's things, especially during the Holidays. For Easter we still wore frilly dresses and bonnets and gloves. Remember, this was during the late fifties. But, oh! At around three years old, Nancy started to renege. She wanted to wear pants like her brothers. She hated it when I would curl her straight hair in curlers. Trying to take her picture at Easter was like pulling teeth if she was in a dress. She would never smile. Of course, she was her Daddy's girl, who seemed to always side in with her.

Moving to the mountain and playing on the farm, she was happiest in overalls or dungarees. Nancy was

five when we made the big move. She was in kindergarten when April Fool's day came around. She
would be six in a few more days. Perhaps to make
better friends, or perhaps just to be more notable, she
told her classmates a story.

"Our family had to move up to the mountains to
a farm that had a very big barn, because we brought
up an elephant that had gone wild at a circus back in
New Jersey."

She told it so realistically that when the teachers
somehow found out about it, they pulled her brothers
out of their classes and took them to the principal's
office to ask about the tale! The boys became absolutely embarrassed, denying the whole story. When
they arrived home, they asked their Dad and me
to make sure Nancy never pulls another stunt like
that! When we confronted her about it, she just said,
nonchalantly, "I didn't mean anything about it, I just
thought it was a good April Fool's joke!" We all did
get quite a chuckle over it.

As Nancy grew older, I never realized that as a
middle child, she felt lonely, and left out of things.
Bill and Ed always did things together, and her
younger brother and sister had each other. I was glad
when Nancy joined the Pioneer Girls, and at age ten,
directed us to a sound church where the Bible was
preached. But, yet, I never detected her melancholy.
Once in a while she would antagonize her younger
brother or sister, I think, now, just to get our attention.
There was even a time when she secretly downed a
bottle of aspirins (at the age of twelve). I took her
to the emergency room to have her stomach pumped

out, thinking this just to be another 'kid' thing to go through. It still didn't register in my mind that it is hard for a middle child to get attention, unless through drastic measures at times. For those of you reading this, please take this to heart if you have a middle child. This has been brought out more now than it was forty years ago. Even though Nancy was saved, did her Bible lessons, was a good school student, usually paid attention to Bill and me, and did her chores around the home and farm, she would still find ways to draw attention in negative ways.

There was a time in the late 60's, early 70's, when riots broke out as young college age students were rebelling. The Woodstock era. The local college had some incidents in Delhi. Nancy was in high school at the time. Word got to me that some of the high school students were lining up to march downtown to meet up with college students in rebellion. If they went, they would all be expelled. Nancy was one of them. I made a mad dash in the car and came into the school parking lot just in time to see the kids starting to make their move. I made my swift move and grabbed Nancy by the shoulder and brought her back into the school to her assigned class with the threat of calling her father home from work. Although very bellig-erent, she obeyed, since she dearly loved her Dad.

Nancy was a very good help to me most of the time. She would have fun with her cousins who came up from New Jersey, and with the Fresh Air Fund children. She was good company for me while helping in the gardens. But I've been writing this chapter to reveal that no matter what change you make, whether you think it's for the better, and this move was, your children can make your heart beat with love and happy times - but they can also break your heart. And, at one time, Nancy broke ours.

The summer before becoming a senior in high school she became a bit infatuated with a boy in our neighborhood. One day she made a statement to me saying, "I would do anything just to keep him and even marry him." But I just laughed it off. Well, she did do something!! She became pregnant. It was a terrible revelation. As I look back, I think now, I was more upset as to how it tarnished my reputation as a parent. I was more concerned about me rather than how this would reflect on my daughter!! George, the father of the baby, was only sixteen - Nancy, seventeen. I could not see such a young man having to get married, but this is what they both wanted. Our pastor did his best to lead George to the Lord and to salvation. He also arranged a sweet, but private wedding in the church for the families. Bill and I arranged a small reception for thirty in, of all places, "Carrolls", which is now, I think, called Burger King, in the town of Oneonta. The hamburger place was quite accommodating, reserving a section just for our little party. There aren't too many places like that used for wedding receptions!!

As for the high school, it had been the policy to expel a student who became pregnant. Nancy was the first who was allowed to stay in school. George was allowed to bring home her work when she became close to her 'time'. Also when the baby was born. A few months later, Nancy graduated.

Through a program called 'Man-Power', George learned about machining and did very well. Since then they have become parents of three children - moved to North Carolina - built their own machine shop and employ eleven people. A few years ago the Charlotte, N.C. Observer newspaper did an article on their success as owners of a small business. They have now been married for thirty-three years.

Next is Thomas. Tom was only twenty-two months when we made the move to the Catskills; therefore he doesn't remember life in New Jersey. Growing up on the farm he became a rather robust and fun loving boy. During the winter his shirt and jacket were always pulled out of his pants and his red belly would be showing from rolling over onto the snow from the toboggan or sled. One time, when about four years old, his younger sister came into the house to tell me, "Tom won't play with me any more! He fell asleep on the ice!" There was a small hill on the front lawn that the kids liked to slide down when it was icy. Tom either fell on a chunk of ice or hit his head on the nearby tree. He wasn't asleep he, was unconscious! By the time I ran to him, he was groggily getting up. That was just one of the times he hit his head while living on the farm.

There was a time when he was either four or five, and he was playing in the yard with his younger sister in early fall; the other children were in school. I went into the house to get laundry from the washing machine to hang outside. In just those few minutes they had disappeared by the time I came back outside! I called and called. - "Tom!" "Thomas!" - "Cathy!"

"Tom! Where are you?!?" Frightened? Of course I was! I first ran to the well on the front lawn. It was high - they couldn't possibly climb into it. But...not in there. I ran to the barn with the hay-mow. Went all through it. Running down to the stream, I kept calling for them. No sign. Raced down the long driveway, crossed over to the pond. Tom had learned how to swim, but no sign of them there. Checking the apple orchard as I ran back to the barn, I thought of them falling through the upper floorboards and unconscious. I finally called Bill to come home. Of course, he's over twenty miles away at work. Another hour went by. Finally, Bill drove into the driveway, and I see two little heads bobbing around in the back seat! My heart never pumped so fast. They had walked over the side hill which was planted with corn that was taller than they were; went down the other side to the macadam road that led to our neighbor farmer, a mile away. As he was preparing to bring them home, Bill drove by. He hailed Bill down, saying, "I think these are yours!" with a big smirk. Can you imagine someone finding a three and four year old walking along a roadway now?? Although back in the mid-sixties a car probably never passed them.

After my nerves calmed, and a few spankings given, (yes, we did spank our children), I was bathing them, and asked Tom, "What made you do such a thing? Why didn't you tell me where you were going?"

His reply, of course, "Well, I knew you wouldn't let us go if we asked. We just wanted to see the cows!"

"Didn't you hear me calling?" His only answer between the tears, "Yes".

Tom was hurt on the head another time when he was, perhaps, six or seven. With permission this time, he was at the same farm with his brothers, who were playing baseball with the farmer's boys, using a lead pipe for a bat! Of all things! You guessed it. Tom was hit over the eye with the pipe. I had to make a mad dash fifteen miles away to our doctor, who checked Tom, and then applied ten or twelve stitches.

When we made the move over to Bovina from that farm, Tom found a job helping another neighbor farmer there. One time Tom was working with the farmer's grandson cleaning out a silo. They were about twelve or fourteen years old at that time. Suddenly, Tom, accidentally, stuck the pitchfork into the top of his foot! Later, as the grandson was telling the story, he laughed heartily, saying, "I couldn't believe Tom didn't say one bad 'cuss' word as we pulled the fork out of his foot!" But that's how Tom was - is. To this day, as far as I know, he still doesn't say, "cuss words".

In high school, Tom played football and was on the wrestling team. It wasn't very easy, as a parent, to watch him get in a tussle and get knocked out on the field. I was made to stay in the bleachers as the first aide attendants worked on him. Before I knew it, he was back on the field.

Tom was a daredevil when it came to driving a car. I never knew what antics he pulled till weeks after his stunts. One, for instance, was when he came home with a very sore foot. He jumped feet first into a swimming hole when he and his friends were at the nearby river, and landed rather hard on a rock. That was his story till I learned later that what he was actually doing was riding on the hood of a car and his friend, the driver, had to stop short. Tom went flying off, and landed on that foot. There was also a time when he gave his father a story about losing a tire off the car because the bolts weren't on tightly. What he and his friends were doing was seeing how fast they could go over a hill to soar over the other side, and came down on that tire and wheel. As for any real problems, I wasn't aware of them. I am sure his brothers and sisters could come up with some interesting stories, if I asked.

After Tom graduated high school, he worked for a while, became married, and then enlisted in the Air Force. While in the service he took courses in electricity and came out of the military five years later. He and his wife, Rita, have been married twenty-six years and now live in Kentucky. Tom manages an electric power plant.

Our youngest child, Cathy, was only six months old when we made the move. She enjoyed living on the farm, but, also enjoyed following and antagonizing her sister, Nancy. When the older children were in school, Cathy and Tom were stuck playing with each other since we had no neighbors for a mile in any direction. When Cathy entered kindergarten, our oldest, Bill, Jr. became a senior in high school. For some reason, she always looked up to her brother, Bill. Perhaps because he was always the first one up on Christmas morning and he would wake her up to go downstairs to see what wonderment was waiting for everyone. We never put up the tree until Christmas Eve, after the younger ones went to bed. I think they still wake each other up on Christmas morning after all these years.

As Cathy grew older she would notice how her sister always wanted to be the proverbial 'tomboy', who never wanted to wear the dresses I made, or bought, for school. At that time, yes, girls wore dresses or skirts, and boys had to wear buttoned down shirts and slacks to school. Cathy shrewdly attained the opposite personality of being more feminine. She agreed to the dresses and having her hair curled and be the sweet thing. Did she get into trouble? I'm sure.

One bad time was when, in her teen years, she and a girlfriend decided that home life was getting to be boring. They ran away. Where to? They left no clue. Bill and I had the police looking for them, as he and one of our sons were also driving around through the night. I stayed home near the phone waiting for the worst, as any mother does. All night, all the next morning. It wasn't like Cathy to do this, but then, I had no idea what was going through her mind. Finally, the call came. "Mom, we want to come home!" She was truly sorry to have created such a problem.

Both of our daughters were rather upset when we changed churches. Bill and I were a bit more strict when it came to wearing certain clothing styles. After all, everyone else was wearing mini-skirts weren't they? Our dating curfews were a bit ridiculous. Their school friends had a bit more freedom. Perhaps that was one of Cathy's problems.

After graduating high school, Cathy became an aide at the local nursing home where I had been working. The home awarded a scholarship each year for a college course in nursing. Cathy became a recipient one year. Praise the Lord! After becoming an L.P.N. she worked a couple more years, then worked her way through college to become a R.N. She now lives in Virginia with her second husband. Working in Roanoke, Cathy manages the offices of Amedisys Home Health Service.

It certainly was a roller coaster ride for Bill and me raising five healthy, robust children in the new environment that even we weren't sure of. It was quite an experience watching each one as they prepared to leave the 'nest'. Even though each child was very different, each one has remarked that they were happy being able to grow up in a rural atmosphere. (Each has admitted to finding ways of getting into trouble.) It blesses me now that they are living Godly lives.

These Catskill Mountain Memories are just some of the many memories and stories that have come to my mind. I pray they have been enjoyable, interesting, educational and whimsical

PLACES TO GO - THINGS TO DO

In and Around The Catskill Mountains

Looking back on the Catskill area, I can think of the many things we did, and the different places we went to. The first thing that comes to mind is the Catskill Game Farm. It's the first place we visited on our trip up from New Jersey when we came to see the farm that was for sale in East Meredith. We had stayed at a motel just off the New York Thruway near Catskill, and after breakfast, we came to the Game Farm. We enjoyed several hours with the animals - petting them - feeding them. Bill was holding one-year-old Tommy at the time (Cathy was not yet born), with a baby bottle sticking out of his hip pocket. It was the funniest thing to see a goat following Bill, trying to get at that milk bottle!! Everyone was getting quite a laugh out of it, not just our family.

All the kids enjoyed the rides at the attraction, also. After leaving the Game Farm and getting nearer to our destination, this was along Rte. 23, we noticed farmers out in their fields plowing, or driving along the highway on their tractors; what attracted us the most was how each one would wave to us. It was quite a drawing card for us to want to move up to the area with such friendliness. Now, 45 years later, do they still wave?? I hope so!

After living on the farm for a while, we started to explore the various areas. We found many places to go swimming other than our own pond. In other chapters I mentioned the East Sidney Dam Park, Bear Spring Mountain Park in Walton, the Otsego Lake in Cooperstown, Gilbert's Lake near Laurens, Minekill Falls in Schoharie. Then there were many places along the banks of the Delaware River and the Susquehanna River. How many people love to go 'tubing' down the Esopus River near Phoenicia? There are numerous lakes and ponds to be found in the Catskill area.

Many of the towns had public swimming pools, most free of charge. Maybe not free any more. We found them in Margaretville, Andes, Delhi, Hobart, Stamford - but the one we frequented the most was in Wilbur Park in Oneonta. It was a great place to celebrate summer birthdays. The kids, and in later years, the grandkids, would swim in the pool while we grown-ups would find a picnic table to set. By the time the sandwiches and salads were put out the kids came running, saying, "We're starved!" After eating they'd go to the playground for a bit, then back to

swimming again. One of us adults would go downtown for a gallon of ice cream and by the time it was
dished out and the birthday cake was on the table, I
think the kids smelled the party fixings because they
were there before the drinks were poured! The most
requested cake I had to make was a chocolate sheet
cake with chocolate icing, and decorated with M &
M's and walnuts. After eating the chocolate, the kids
had to go back in the pool showers to clean off before
they were allowed in the cars.

During the winter there was, and still is, so much
snow fun. I'll begin with the ski areas. The nearest
place to us, when we moved over to Bovina, was
the Bobcat Ski Center in Andes. About 15 years ago
there were at least 18 trails there. Are there more
now? I don't really know. Belleayre Mountain is
in Highmount, Plattekill Mountain Ski Center is in
Roxbury, Deer Run Resort is in Stamford, and there
is skiing in Windham, and on Hunter Mountain.
Hunter is a very popular place with something going
on year-round with its various festivals. Our family
was not one for skiing though. Sledding and tobogganing was quite the winter sport for us since we had
quite a few of our own hills to have fun on. When
friends and relatives came for some winter fun,
there were always a few trails ready for the kids to
go down on. Not just short runs. They made trails
down the hill through the hayfields, around the trees,
across the streams, and the pond when it was frozen.
As they grew older, that fun wore off and the boys
began to think of snowmobiles. Tom was the daring
one, trying to find the steepest hills to ride down on.

There were many good times when the neighbors would get together in the evenings and ride trails up in the woods and fields. Sometimes you could see a dozen snow mobile headlights, one behind another, on a distant hill in the dark of night. There were times they would stop at our house for hot chocolate and whatever I had made - cookies, cup- cakes, etc. Other times the bunch of them would visit some other home. And, now, 15 years later, I hear of my nieces and nephews who have bought some land in the Catskills with one of the main reasons is to go snow-mobiling. The whole area is a four-season wonderland.

Then, there is the pleasure of camping. Of course, our family did our own thing on our own property, (except for those times we took our vacations in the south). Many times Bill would have a huge camp-fire going for family and friends, or Sunday School groups, or Boy Scouts - where we could roast hot-dogs, and marshmallows for those ever popular s'mores. Notable state parks were East Sidney Dam, Chenango Valley, Oquaga Creek, Gilbert Lake, Max Shaul, - other places were in Jefferson Heights, Lew Beach, Ashokan Reservoir, Hunt's Pond, and Pioneer Trails in Delancey. I know there must be many more.

The summer season was, and still is, the busiest season in and around the Catskills. When we lived there, no one needed cell phones, computers, I-pods, game-boys, etc. Just imagination. Some farms turned into vacation ranches. Horseback riding being the main attraction. While walking mountain trails you never knew when you would meet up with a group out on horses. At times we had to be careful of ATVs (all terrain vehicles) - most people were rather careful with their driving, though.

A few yearly events come to mind, other than small town parades and picnics. One event was on Memorial Day Weekend - the canoe races on the Susquehanna River from Cooperstown to Bainbridge. One time while waiting on the banks of the river in Bainbridge for the first of the canoers to arrive, we were sitting with quite a few people. Some were walking their dogs on leashes. But one of the more comical sights was to see a man with a small pink pig on a leash!!

Usually in the middle of July, the Saint James Episcopal Church on Rte. 28, in Lake Delaware, held an arts and crafts and antiques fair. I would rent a table at the affair while living in Bovina to sell my crafts and collectibles. But I had the most success in selling our cultivated raspberries, which would be just ripening. Bill and I would hurry and pick maybe two dozen quart baskets full in the early morning from our raspberry patch near our vegetable garden. By the time we set them on the table they'd be gone in minutes, before the gates were opened, bought by the other vendors at $2.00 a quart. Bill would drive back to the farm, strip all the ripe berries off the branches, and hurry back with perhaps another eight or ten quart baskets full. And again, the vendors would scoop them up for themselves. I'm sure that now a half pint would be about $2.00. It seemed that every year many people, locals and visitors, looked forward to the St. James affair - it was always crowded - if for nothing else but the wonderful chili served by those working in the kitchen. As far as I know, St. James still holds that yearly event.

The teen week of August was always full of excitement. It was the week of the Delaware County Fair in Walton. A big event the kids always looked forward to. We all enjoyed strolling around to see the animals, fowl, tractors, old time cars and trucks, etc. Then later, to see who had been awarded ribbons. Of course, we always had to walk the length of the Midway with its clowns, horror house, fun house, and places to spend our quarters to try to win a prize. We'd spend $5.00 worth of quarters to win a 50 cent prize. Wasn't that always the way it was, though? The aromas of the sausage, peppers, onions, hotdogs, and funnel cakes were quite the draw, also. By the time we walked the whole place our feet would be drag-ging, but there always seemed to be one more thing to see. Other counties had their fairs, too, but living in Delaware County, we always found ourselves in Walton. Once in a great while we would go to the State Fair.

One year, after our 'nest' was empty, we took our neighbors, Mike and Rose, to the fair in the after-noon to watch "tractor-pulls". A noisy, dusty, but fun thing to watch. About half way to Walton, it was just after noon, Bill was traveling the speed limit on the highway, and out of no-where, a large deer ran across the road from the left side in front of us!! Bill couldn't stop in time and the impact released the hood of the car and broke the headlights, killing the deer, which bounced off into the ditch on the right. We were rounding a curve where it would be too dangerous to stop the car, but a few yards ahead; Bill did stop to make sure the animal was dead. Fortunately, the car kept running, but with the hood up on the windshield, Bill could only see the yellow lines in the middle of the road out of his driver's side window. Driving approximately a half-mile we saw a gas station on the left. Mike got out of the car and directed Bill over to it. There were some men there that Bill talked to about the mishap - telling them it was a four point buck - they could have the deer, Bill was too upset to claim it since our car was just purchased, brand new, a couple months before!! We were supposed to report the incident to the Sheriff's Dept., but that was ten miles back in the opposite direction in Delhi. Being Saturday, Bill figured there would only be a skeleton crew on anyway; -and he wanted to see the tractor-pulls first, since we knew a couple of the drivers. The men at the gas station gave him some rope to tie down the hood and said they would take care of the deer. Off we went to the Walton Fair! Mike was the one who continued to be upset! About every fifteen minutes he would say to Bill, "How can you sit here watching these tractors while you should be reporting the accident? You will get a fine!!" Bill would calm him down each time and just enjoyed the pulls. When Mike would jump up to say something even Rose tried to tell him Bill would take care of things. The poor man...for me it was more fun to watch him than the tractors. Eventually, when it was over, we arrived at the police station around 4:30 P.M. Bill went in to make the report, Mike went in also. The papers were signed to bring to our insurance agent after the weekend, and everything was settled in a matter of minutes. Being from the 'city', Mike couldn't get over the fact that not only Bill, but the desk Sergeant was so laid back taking care of the whole report, as if it was just another mundane happening...which it was. How many reports do the police get of deer being hit on the roads and highways in the Catskills? Quite a few!

Other places to go to and see would be the Hanford Mills in east Meredith, the Stone Fort Museum in Schoharie, Howes cave, the Baseball Hall of fame in Cooperstown, the Farmers museum in Cooperstown, the Soccer Hall of Fame in Oneonta. I remember taking grand-kids to Arkville for a ride on the Delaware and Ulster Rail Ride, I'm assuming that is still open.

When we moved over to Bovina from East Meredith, we left our wonderful apple orchard behind, also the many blueberry bushes in the wild. We then planted over a hundred blueberry bushes to have for our own. As for apples, we found Schoharie Valley was a wonderful place to go for a drive out on Rte. 30, and up to Schoharie where there were 'pick-your-own' apple orchards. The trip there was well worth it, to be able to pick many different varieties of apples and come home with baskets or feed bags full of the delicious fruits. Naturally Bill and I would always reward ourselves and whatever kids were with us to dinner somewhere along the long route home. We found strawberry fields out there also. I can't begin to tell you how many strawberries we had picked each year. And I know the 'city' folk enjoyed picking them, also. I met and talked with many who couldn't wait to bring the fresh, wonderfully tasting, berries back home to their city friends. Usually, if it was warm enough, I'd let the kids go for a swim in the Schoharie near Middleburg where there was a little park and 'swimming hole' after picking berries, then head to a place to eat. Is the Turtle Rock Café still there??

Although I had a large vegetable garden at home I could always go through the valley and find something I hadn't grown at one of the many stands. There was a carrot farm where anyone could go in and harvest whatever carrots were left in the field after the farmer plucked out what he could with his machinery. Usually, the carrots that were left were rather big and tough, but one year Bill and I thought they would be good for the pigs we were raising. We dug up 2 large burlap bags full, and getting home, I threw a handful in to the pigs. They smelled them, bit into them, and walked away from them. Ungrateful pigs!! I thought. The next day I decided to cook a pot-full for the ungrateful pigs....perhaps they were too tough for them, also. Putting the cooled, cooked carrots in their 'slop' trough, the pigs had them gone in minutes! And were looking for more. Every afternoon when Bill came home from work he'd see the pot of carrots cooling on the stove and wondered what he would be getting for supper. Those cooked carrots went so well that we drove to the farm again and dug up a couple more burlap bags full of the big orange veggies. No, that winter our hams and pork chops weren't orange, and they didn't taste like carrots either. But, those carrots did help with the feed bill, though.

Perhaps this has helped you to get up and go and check out the various places in the Catskill Mountains. I hope you can find your own favorite places to explore and lure you to not only vacation at, but to find your own little nest along a creek in a valley or on a mountain top and settle in for a while.

Biography:

B orn and raised on a dairy farm in Avenel, New Jersey, Catherine felt rather closed in after she married and had five children. She and her husband, Bill, were living with their family in Carteret, a fast developing town in N.J. He was a policeman, but she was able to talk him into leaving his job and move to the Catskill Mountains in upstate New York.

Always jotting down certain memorable times, she would send articles that were published in Catskill Country and Grit Magazine.

As the children started to leave the nest, Catherine took correspondence courses and received certificates of completion from "The Special Publishing Course" of the Institute of Children's Literature, and also from "Christian Writing Techniques" of the Christian Writers Institute.

Catherine also has certificates from Liberty University in Lynchburg, Virginia, stating that she is a graduate of their correspondence courses of its Institute of Biblical Studies and The Life Of Christ.

Now a widow and living in Ocala, Florida, she has been putting together her memories of living in the Catskill Mountains.

Catherine M. (Den Bleyker) Troost
2805 S.E. 110th St. lot B-36,
Ocala, Fl. 34480

9 781607 910718